ALWAYS ON

SEAMLESS SUPPORT AROUND THE CLOCK

UNLOCK THE POTENTIAL OF A 24X7 SERVICE DESK AND EMPOWER YOUR BUSINESS WITH UNINTERRUPTED SUPPORT SOLUTIONS.

JAYASHANKAR LINGAIAH

ISBN

Hardcase 979-8-89673-354-6
Paperback 979-8-89544-823-6

Dedication

To the countless service desk professionals whose tireless efforts keep businesses running smoothly and to those striving to make a difference every day—this book is for you.

Contents

Chapter 1: Understanding the Service Desk 23

- **What is a Service Desk?**

  - Definition and Purpose
  - Different Types of Service Desks (IT, Customer Support, etc.)

- **Importance of a Service Desk in IT Infrastructure**

  - Role & Benefits of Service Desk

Chapter 2: Service Desk Fundamentals 30

- **Key Functions of a Service Desk**

  - Incident Management

Chapter 8: Case Studies and Real-World Examples 178

- **Success Stories**

    - Examples of Effective Service Desks

- **Lessons Learned from Challenges**

    - Common Pitfalls and How to Avoid Them

Acknowledgments

I extend my heartfelt gratitude to my parents, Smt. Ningajamma R and Sri. Lingaiah SM, for their unwavering blessings and support since my birth.

To my wife, Leela, and my daughter, Aadvika, your love, patience, and encouragement have been my greatest source of strength—thank you for always being there for me.

I am deeply grateful to my coach, Dr. Manjunath M.S. Sir, for his invaluable inspiration, guidance, and support, which played a pivotal role in turning my dream of publishing this book into reality.

A special thanks to my manager and mentor, Praveen Kumar Desai, for his continuous guidance, motivation, and support in shaping my service desk career.

I extend heartfelt thanks to my dear friend and well-wisher, Girish Kumar, for standing by me steadfastly through all the ups and downs of life.

I am also grateful to my whole family, colleagues, and friends, whose direct and indirect support has been instrumental in this journey.

To my Diamond CBL friends, your unwavering encouragement and inspiration have been invaluable in helping me embrace challenges and push boundaries—thank you.

Finally, I am deeply thankful to Notion Press for their professional guidance and unwavering support throughout the publishing process of this book.

Thank you all!

Preface

Dear Readers,

Welcome to the world of 24x7 IT service desk management. In this digital era where technology never sleeps and global operations demand seamless support around the clock, the role of the IT service desk has never been more critical. Whether it's resolving a midnight system outage, guiding a user through a complex application issue, or ensuring the continuous availability of critical services, the IT service desk is the backbone of modern business continuity.

This book is born out of twelve years of hands-on experience, facing the challenges and triumphs that come with managing an around-the-clock service desk. Throughout my career, I have navigated the evolving landscape of IT support, witnessing firsthand the shift from traditional office hours to the relentless demands of a 24x7 environment. This journey has provided invaluable insights, which I am eager to share with you.

The aim of this book is not only to provide practical guidance but also to inspire and equip both new and seasoned service desk managers with the tools they need to succeed. We will explore strategies for building a resilient and responsive service desk team, implementing effective processes, and leveraging technology to enhance service delivery. By delving into real-life scenarios and case studies, I hope to offer a realistic and relatable perspective on the complexities of managing a 24x7 operation.

Uniquely, this book emphasizes the human aspect of service desk management. Technology may be at the heart of IT support, but it is the people—the dedicated professionals behind the scenes—who make it all possible. Therefore, we will discuss ways to foster a positive and productive work environment, manage stress, and maintain team morale in a high-pressure setting.

As you embark on this journey, remember that every challenge is an opportunity for growth. The strategies and insights presented in this book are designed to help you navigate the dynamic world of IT service desk management with confidence and expertise.

Thank you for choosing this book as your guide. I hope it serves as a valuable resource in your quest to provide exceptional 24x7 IT support. Let's embark on this journey together and redefine what it means to deliver outstanding service in a non-stop world.

Warm regards,
Jayashankar Lingaiah

Foreword

If you've ever wondered how a 24x7 service desk can revolutionize your business operations or how seamless support can drive success, then *Always On: Seamless Support Around the* Clock by Jayashankar Lingaiah is the book you've been looking for. Written with expert insight and practical guidance, this book is your ultimate resource for harnessing the power of continuous IT support to elevate your business to new heights.

As a Mind Performance Coach and the author of the bestseller *Unleash the Power of Reading*, I have seen firsthand the profound impact that discipline and positive routines can have on one's life. In a world overflowing with distractions and demands, maintaining focus and building lasting habits can often feel overwhelming. *Always On* offers the clarity and guidance you need to navigate these challenges and build a robust IT support system that drives business success.

This book is not just about setting up a service desk or implementing technical solutions; it's about creating a resilient and efficient support operation capable of adapting to the demands of a 24x7 world. With every chapter, you will uncover actionable insights and best practices for managing a service desk team, leveraging technology, and maintaining high service standards. From designing effective shift patterns to utilizing advanced tools, *Always On* provides a comprehensive roadmap to help you optimize your IT support and achieve operational excellence.

In today's environment, where every moment counts and customer expectations are high, this book serves as a beacon for achieving seamless service delivery. It's about understanding the principles of continuous support and applying them to create a service desk that aligns with your business goals. With practical advice on team management, knowledge systems, and technological advancements, *Always On* empowers you to enhance your support operations and deliver exceptional customer experiences.

Whether you're looking to streamline your support processes, improve team performance, or stay ahead of technological trends, *Always On* is your essential guide. This book promises not only to inform you but also to inspire you to take actionable steps toward a more effective and efficient 24x7 service desk.

Here's to mastering the art of continuous support and unlocking the full potential of your IT operations. I am excited to see the positive impact this book will have on your journey toward service excellence and business success.

Best Wishes,

Manjunath MS
MIND PERFORMANCE COACH

Dr. Manjunath
Mind Performance Coach
Author of *Unleash the Power of Reading*

About the Author

Jayashankar Lingaiah

Service Desk & Service Delivery Manager, ITIL, PMP, SCRUM MASTER certified professional

Professional Background

Jayashankar Lingaiah is a seasoned IT service desk manager with over 18 years of experience in the IT industry. Throughout his career, he has managed diverse teams and overseen numerous projects, ensuring seamless IT support and enhancing user satisfaction. Jayashankar holds a BE in Computer Science, demonstrating a deep understanding of IT service management best practices.

Career Highlights

- **Leadership in IT Service Desk Management:** Successfully managed a team of 15 service desk analysts supporting customers across the IT infrastructure support business.

- **Process Improvement:**Implemented a ticketing system to manage global support operations and extensively involved in annual process improvement reviews.

- **Incident and Problem Management:**Played a key role in implementing process flows for incident and problem management as per ITIL standards.

- **Customer Focus:**Fostered strong relationships with stakeholders and users, continuously improving service delivery to meet their expectations.

Personal Philosophy

Jayashankar believes that a successful IT service desk is built on the pillars of effective communication, continuous learning, and a user-centric approach. He is dedicated to creating environments where service desk professionals can thrive, innovate, and provide exceptional support.

Beyond the Desk

Outside of his professional life, Jayashankar enjoys music, movies, outdoor sports, and trekking, which he believes contribute to a well-rounded and balanced approach to work and life.

Connect with Jayashankar Lingaiah

- **LinkedIn:**www.linkedin.com/in/jayashankar-lingaiah-81491418

- **Email:**jayashankarkol@gmail.com

Welcome and Introduction

Purpose of the Book

The purpose of this book is to guide you through the fundamentals of service desk concepts in a simple and accessible manner. It covers all the essential aspects, including processes and best practices, involved in setting up and running a service desk team, particularly within an IT infrastructure environment.

With clear explanations, practical advice, and real-life examples, this book aims to equip new service desk managers with the knowledge and skills needed to deliver exceptional customer service, manage incidents efficiently, and foster continuous learning and improvement.

Whether you are new to the Service Desk Manager or Analyst role or looking to enhance your skills, this book offers valuable insights to help you grow and succeed in service desk management.

Who This Book is For

This book is intended for a diverse audience:

1. **Graduates and Professional Graduates**: Those who aspire to pursue a career in IT service desk management.

2. **New Service Desk Analysts**: Individuals seeking to learn and enhance their knowledge in the field.

3. **Service Desk Managers**: Professionals looking to grow and advance in their careers.

4. **IT Infrastructure Leaders**: Those involved in IT service delivery management who want to deepen their understanding of service desk operations.

Overview of the Content

This book provides a comprehensive insight into the service desk, covering:

1. **Definition and Types**: An overview of what a service desk is and the different types that exist.

2. **Role in Business**: The critical role a service desk plays in business operations.

3. **Benefits**: The advantages of implementing a service desk.

4. **Process and best practices** – Covers all the process and best practices for 24X7 IT service desk.

Additionally, it outlines the steps to set up and manage a service desk to enhance team productivity and improve customer experience.

The book also covers the use of service management tools to measure key metrics and KPIs, helping to achieve business goals and make informed decisions for growth.

Chapter 1

Understanding the Service Desk

1. **What is a Service Desk?**

   o **Definition and Purpose**

A Service Desk is a function or department within an organization dedicated to supporting IT service users. Serving as the initial point of contact for IT incidents and requests, it typically operates in shifts to provide support to users across different time zones.

Purpose – The primary purpose of service desk include.

1. **Incident management:** Resolving or handling the incidents which include restoring the IT services back to normal or working conditions as soon as possible. Incident can be any unplanned service interruption or degradation in the quality of service.

2. **Service Request Management:** Managing service requests like access requests, password reset, account unlock etc., mainly non-incident related requests.

3. **Problem Management:** working on root cause analysis for critical/major incidents and recurring incidents.

4. **Change Management:** Assisting on change management on need basis to reduce the incidents or service disruptions.

5. **Communication:** Single point of contact for all communications related to outages, incidents and all the requests between IT organizations and users.

6. **Service Improvements**: Feedback gathering from end users and analyzing the incident trend and proposing a improvement in service.

7. **Knowledge Management:** creating, maintaining, and sharing knowledge articles with end user to resolve the basic incidents and learning within team.

Key Components-

1. **Ticketing system:** Used to log, track, and manage the incident and all other requests. Also, for generating reports for various delivery aspects.

2. **Knowledgebase:** A centralized repository to create and manage knowledge articles which help users and service desk team to resolve the basic common issues.

3. **Self-service portal:** A web interface where user can log, track and manage their tickets and also can access self-help information's.

Different Types of Service Desks (IT, Customer Support, etc.)

Types of service desks are designed and categorized based on the business function they support or types of users they support.

1. **IT Service Desk**

   - Purpose – Provide support to IT services issues like software, hardware, network, and other technical issues. Refer definition and purpose section for more details.

2. **Customer Service Desk**

   - Purpose – Support end customers with their queries and complaints on products or services. Product info, order tracking, return and refund and technical support.

3. **HR Service Desk**

   - Purpose – Supporting employees on HR relates issues and enquiries. Benefits and compensation, Employee onboarding and payroll etc.

4. **Facilities Service Desk**

   - Purpose – Support and answer facility related queries and concerns. Maintenance request, space management, health & safety issues, and office supply management.

5. **Finance Service Desk**

   - Purpose: Assist with financial issues and enquiries like invoice, expense, budget, and policy guidance.

6. **Educational Service Desk**

   - Purpose: Provide support for students, faculty, and staff in Enrollment and registration, academic records, library and research in educational institutions.

7. **Healthcare Service Desk**

   - Purpose: Support healthcare professionals and patients with electronic health record, appointment scheduling, medical billing inquiries, etc.

8. **Sales and Marketing Service Desk**

   - Purpose: Assist sales and marketing teams with their marketing campaign, sales data, lead management, etc.

2. Role and Benefits of service desk

The service desk is a vital component of any service delivery operation, especially within IT infrastructure. It serves as a single point of contact for customers and the service delivery team, facilitating efficient and effective delivery.

The service desk team is responsible for tracking and managing incidents, problems, and service requests until closure. They also oversee SLAs/SLTs related to service delivery using ticketing systems, keeping all internal and external stakeholders informed on updates.

Available 24/7, the service desk provides support across different time zones, ensuring continuous assistance.

1. Improved Efficiency and Productivity

   - **Quick Resolution:** Faster resolution of IT issues minimizes downtime and allows employees to remain productive.

- **Automation:** Automating routine tasks and requests reduces manual workload and speeds up service delivery.

2. Enhanced User Experience

- **Single Point of Contact:** Users have a clear and consistent point of contact for all IT-related issues, improving their overall experience.

- **Proactive Support:** Proactively addresses potential issues before they become critical, enhancing user satisfaction.

3. Better Incident and Problem Management

- **Incident Tracking**: Systematic tracking and management of incidents ensure timely resolution and minimal business disruption.

- **Problem Identification:** Identifies root causes of recurring issues, preventing them from reoccurring and improving long-term stability.

4. Resource Optimization

- **Cost Management:** Helps optimize IT resource use, reducing waste and controlling costs associated with IT services.

- **Performance Monitoring:** Tracks and analyzes performance metrics, identifying areas for improvement and ensuring efficient use of resources.

5. Performance Monitoring and Continuous Improvement

- **Metrics and KPIs:** Tracks performance against key performance indicators (KPIs), providing insights into service quality and areas for improvement.

- **Continuous Improvement:** Uses performance data to identify trends, improve processes, and enhance service delivery.

Chapter Summary – Mindmap

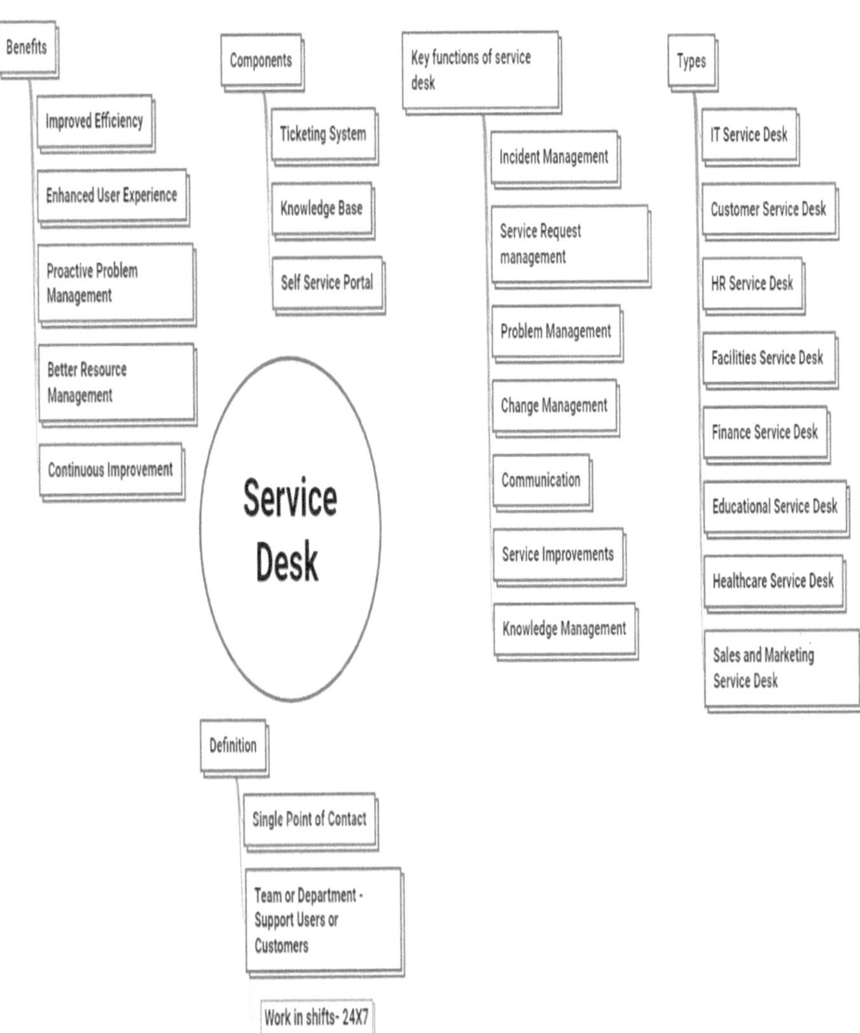

Chapter 2

Service Desk Fundamentals

Key functions of service desk:

A service desk plays a crucial role in ensuring the smooth operation and effectiveness of IT services within an organization. The main functions of a service desk include the following:

1. Incident Management

- **Incident Logging:** Captures and categorizes incidents reported by users, as well as those identified through proactive monitoring.

- **Incident Resolution:** Aims to quickly diagnose and resolve incidents to restore normal service operations.

- **Incident Escalation:** Refers incidents to higher-level support teams when necessary for resolution.

- **Incident Tracking:** Continuously monitors the status of incident resolution and keeps users informed throughout the process.

2. Service Request Management

- **Request Fulfillment:** Oversees the management and fulfillment of user service requests, such as access to software, hardware, or information.

- **Request Logging:** Documents and categorizes all service requests made by users.
- **Request Tracking:** Keeps track of the progress of request fulfillment to ensure timely and efficient completion.

3. Problem Management

- **Problem Identification:** Focuses on identifying critical and recurring incidents as candidates for deeper investigation.
- **Root Cause Analysis:** Conducts thorough investigations to determine the underlying causes of problems, aiming to prevent recurrence.
- **Problem Resolution:** Develops and implements permanent solutions to resolve identified problems and mitigate future incidents.
- **Problem Tracking:** Monitors the entire process of problem resolution, ensuring proper documentation and follow-through.

4. Access Management

- **Access Request Approval:** Ensures that all access requests are properly authorized by the relevant authorities before being granted.
- **User Provisioning:** Involves creating and setting up new user accounts, assigning appropriate access rights based on roles and responsibilities.
- **Password Management:** Assists users with password resets and enforces strong password policies to maintain security.

- **Access Issue Resolution:** Troubleshoots and resolves issues related to user access, ensuring minimal disruption to users' tasks.

Incident Management

An incident is defined as an unplanned interruption or reduction in the quality of a service. Examples include application outages, inaccessible websites, or unresponsive reports. Incident Management is a vital function within the service desk, aiming to restore normal service operations as swiftly as possible to mitigate business impact. The following outlines the key components and processes of Incident Management:

1. Incident Identification and Logging

- **Detection:** Incidents may be identified by end-users, IT staff, or through monitoring tools. Any event that disrupts or poses a risk to service continuity is considered an incident.

- **Logging:** Every incident is documented in the Incident Management system, capturing details such as a description of the incident, time of occurrence, user information, and the impact on services.

2. Categorization and Prioritization

- **Categorization:** Incidents are classified according to their type (e.g., hardware, software, network) to streamline handling and reporting processes.

- **Service Level Agreements (SLAs):** SLAs agreed with stakeholders, the expected response and resolution timelines for different incident types, ensuring they are resolved within agreed-upon timeframes.

- **Prioritization:** Incidents are assigned priority levels based on their urgency and the extent of their impact on business operations. Typical priority levels include:

  - **High Priority:** Incidents with critical business impact or major service disruptions.

  - **Medium Priority:** Incidents with significant impact, though not critical.

  - **Low Priority:** Incidents that cause minor disruptions with limited business impact.

3. Initial Diagnosis and Escalation

- **Initial Diagnosis:** The service desk conducts an initial assessment to attempt to resolve the incident using known solutions or available workarounds.

- **Escalation:** If the service desk cannot resolve the incident at the first level, it is escalated to a more specialized support team.

4. Investigation and Diagnosis

- **Detailed Analysis:** The assigned support team performs an in-depth investigation to diagnose the incident, aiming to either resolve the issue or provide an effective workaround.

- **Resource Allocation:** The necessary resources and expertise are mobilized to ensure the incident is resolved efficiently.

5. Resolution and Recovery

- **Solution Implementation:** Upon identifying the cause, a solution is applied to restore normal service operations.

- **Verification:** The solution undergoes testing to confirm that it resolves the incident without introducing new issues.

6. Incident Closure

- **User Confirmation:** Before closing the incident, confirmation is obtained from the user to ensure their issue has been fully resolved.

- **Documentation:** Detailed records of the incident, including the resolution process, are documented for future reference and analysis.

7. Communication

- **Status Updates:** Users and stakeholders are kept informed of the incident's status, estimated resolution time, and any temporary workarounds.

- **Post-Incident Communication:** Once the incident is resolved, users are briefed on the cause and the steps taken to prevent recurrence.

8. Post-Incident Review

- **Analysis:** A thorough review is conducted for major incidents to determine what went wrong and to extract valuable lessons learned.

- **Improvement:** Recommendations are made for process enhancements and preventive measures based on the review findings.

9. Metrics and Reporting

- **Performance Metrics:** Key performance indicators (KPIs) such as incident response times, resolution times, and user satisfaction levels are tracked.

- **Reporting:** Regular reports are generated to offer insights into incident trends, service desk performance, and potential areas for improvement.

10. Continuous Improvement

- **Feedback Integration:** Incident data and user feedback are utilized to drive continuous enhancements in the Incident Management process.

- **Training:** Service desk staff receive ongoing training and participate in knowledge-sharing activities to improve their problem-solving abilities and efficiency.

Benefits of Effective Incident Management:

- **Reduced Downtime:** Swift incident resolution minimizes business disruption and service downtime.

- **Increased User Satisfaction:** Effective handling and clear communication bolster user confidence and satisfaction.

- **Optimized Resource Utilization:** Strategic prioritization and categorization ensure that resources are used effectively.

- **Enhanced Service Quality:** Continuous improvement efforts lead to more reliable and higher-quality IT services.

- **Proactive Problem Management:** Insights from incident data facilitate the early identification and resolution of underlying issues.

Service Request Management

Service requests encompass a wide range of user needs, from simple inquiries to complex issues, enhancements, or even new developments. Larger, more intricate service requests often adopt a project management approach to ensure their successful completion.

1. Logging and Categorization of Requests

- **Request Logging:** When users submit service requests through various channels like phone, email, or web portals, these requests are recorded in the service management system.

- **Categorization:** Each request is classified by type (e.g., enhancements, access requests, information requests) to streamline processing and facilitate reporting.

2. Prioritization of Requests

- **Urgency and Impact Assessment:** Service requests are prioritized based on their urgency and the extent of their impact on business operations, with high-priority requests affecting critical operations being addressed first.

- **Adherence to Service Level Agreements (SLAs):** SLAs outline the expected response and resolution times for different types of requests, ensuring they are managed within the agreed-upon timeframes.

3. Verification and Approval Process

- **Initial Verification:** The validity and completeness of the request are confirmed, ensuring all necessary information is provided.

- **Approval Workflow:** Certain requests, such as those involving access to sensitive data or significant IT infrastructure changes, may require authorization from designated personnel before proceeding.

4. Fulfillment of Requests

- **Standard Operating Procedures:** Requests are handled according to standardized procedures and predefined workflows, promoting consistency and efficiency.

- **Resource Allocation:** The necessary resources (e.g., software licenses, hardware components) and personnel are assigned to fulfill the request effectively.

- **Interdepartmental Coordination:** Some requests may require collaboration with other departments or teams, such as coordinating with facilities management for hardware installations.

5. Communication and User Updates

- **Ongoing Status Updates:** Users are regularly informed about the progress of their requests, including expected completion times and any potential delays.

- **Final Notification:** Upon fulfillment, users receive a notification that their request has been completed, along with any relevant instructions for using the provided services or resources.

6. Request Closure

- **User Satisfaction Confirmation:** Before closing the request, confirmation is obtained from the user to ensure their needs have been fully met.

- **Comprehensive Documentation:** Detailed records of the request and the steps taken to fulfill it are documented for future reference and analysis.

7. Post-Fulfillment Review

- **Quality Assurance:** A review is conducted to ensure the request was fulfilled accurately and meets the required standards.

- **Feedback Collection:** User feedback is gathered to evaluate satisfaction levels and identify opportunities for improvement.

8. Metrics and Reporting

- **Tracking Performance Metrics:** Key performance indicators (KPIs), such as request fulfillment time, user satisfaction, and the volume of processed requests, are closely monitored.

- **Regular Reporting:** Detailed reports are generated to offer insights into request trends, service desk performance, and areas that may need enhancement.

9. Continuous Process Improvement

- **Regular Process Review:** The Request Fulfillment process is periodically reviewed and updated to improve efficiency and effectiveness.

- **Ongoing Training and Knowledge Sharing:** Continuous training is provided to service desk staff, while best practices and lessons learned are shared to elevate service delivery standards.

Benefits of Efficient Request Fulfillment:

- **Enhanced Efficiency:** Standardized workflows and procedures streamline the request-handling process, reducing the time and effort required.

- **Higher User Satisfaction:** Prompt and accurate fulfillment of requests enhances user satisfaction and trust in the service desk.

- **Optimized Resource Utilization:** Effective resource allocation ensures that requests are fulfilled without unnecessary delays or additional costs.

- **Improved Service Quality:** Continuous improvements lead to higher quality and reliability in the IT services provided.

- **Effective Communication:** Regular updates and clear communication keep users informed, reducing uncertainty and enhancing their overall experience.

Common Types of Service Requests:

- **Access Requests:** For access to systems and applications.

- **Information Requests:** For information or documentation.

- **Hardware Requests:** For new or replacement hardware.

- **Software Requests:** For software installations, updates, or licenses.

- **Software Enhancements:** To add new functionalities or modify existing ones to align with business needs.

- **Password Resets:** For resetting passwords.

- **Administrative Changes:** For updates to user profiles, permissions, or settings.

Problem Management

Problem Management is a crucial function within the service desk, dedicated to investigating and identifying the root causes of recurring incidents and major issues that significantly impact business operations. This process aims to find permanent solutions to reduce the frequency of these incidents, ultimately enhancing the stability and availability of IT services.

1. Problem Identification

- **Identify Proactively:** Problems are identified proactively through methods like trend analysis, monitoring, and other predictive detection strategies before they result in incidents.

- **Through Incident Management:** Problems are also identified and logged by analyzing patterns in recurring incidents or significant issues with greater business impact that have already occurred.

2. Logging and Categorizing Problems

- **Detailed Logging:** Problems are recorded in detail in the Problem Management system, including comprehensive details such as problem descriptions, affected services, impacts, and any linked incidents.

- **Systematic Categorization:** Problems are categorized based on their characteristics (e.g., hardware, software, network), for better management and reporting.

3. Prioritizing Problems

- **Evaluating Urgency and Impact:** Problems are prioritized according to their urgency and potential impact on business operations, with those affecting critical services being addressed first.

- **Service Level Agreements (SLAs):** SLAs agreed with stakeholders, the expected response and resolution timelines for different problem types, ensuring they are resolved within agreed-upon timeframes.

4. Conducting Root Cause Analysis (RCA)

- **Thorough Investigation:** An detailed investigation is performed to determine the root cause of the problem, often requiring collaboration with multiple IT teams and key stakeholders.

- **Tools & Techniques:** Techniques like the "5 Whys" and the Fishbone Diagram (Ishikawa) are employed to identify the underlying cause of the problem.

5. Managing Workarounds and Known Errors

- **Providing Interim Solutions:** Temporary workarounds are provided to mitigate the problem's impact while a permanent solution is being implemented, often managed as part of incident management.

- **Update Known Errors:** Problems with identified root causes and available workarounds are updated as known errors in the Knowledge Management system for future reference.

6. Resolving Problems

- **Implementing Permanent Solutions:** A lasting solution is implemented to resolve the problem and prevent its recurrence. This may involve modifications to hardware, software, processes, or configurations.

- **Coordinated Implementation:** The solution is rolled out in alignment with Change Management protocols to avoid introducing new issues or disruptions.

7. Closing Problems

- **Testing and Confirmation:** The solution is rigorously tested to ensure that it fully resolves the underlying problem without damaging the working functionalities.

- **Thorough Documentation:** Detailed records of the problem, its root cause, the solution, and any associated incidents are maintained for future analysis and reference.

- **Communicating Resolution:** Users and stakeholders are promptly informed about the resolution of the problem and any preventive measures to follow to avoid the recurrence.

8. Reviewing and Learning from Problems

- **Post – Analysis:** A review is conducted for significant problems to evaluate what went wrong, how it was resolved, and the lessons learned from the experience.

- **Process Improvements:** Recommendations for process enhancements and preventive actions are identified from the review's findings to prevent future occurrences.

9. Tracking Performance and Reporting

- **Monitoring Key Metrics:** Key performance indicators (KPIs) such as the time taken to resolve problems, the recurrence of incidents, and the number of problems identified and resolved are closely tracked.

- **Detailed Reports:** Regular reports are generated to provide insights into problem trends, the effectiveness of the service desk, and improvement opportunities.

10. Driving Continuous Improvement

- **Process Optimization Regularly:** The Problem Management process is regularly reviewed and refined to improve its efficiency and effectiveness.

- **Regular Training and Knowledge Sharing:** Continuous training and knowledge sharing are encouraged among service desk and IT staff, with best practices and lessons learned adapted to improve the Problem Management capabilities.

Advantages of Effective Problem Management:

- **Incident Recurrence Reduction:** By addressing root causes, Problem Management significantly decreases the frequency of recurring incidents, resulting in lesser service disruptions.

- **Increased Service Stability:** Resolving the underlying causes of problems contributes to the increased stability and reliability of IT services.

- **Improved User Experience:** Minimizing the occurrence and impact of incidents fosters greater user satisfaction and trust in IT services.

- **Cost-Efficient Operations:** By preventing incidents and reducing their impact, the overall cost of IT operations and support is lowered.

- **Proactive Approach:** Shifting from reactive to proactive management of IT issues leads to better preparedness and faster response times.

Key Problem Management Techniques:

- **Root Cause Analysis (RCA):** A systematic approach to investigate and identify the fundamental cause of a problem.

- **The "5 Whys":** A tool or technique involving repeated questioning to drill down to the root cause of a problem.

- **Fishbone Diagram (Ishikawa):** A visual tool that help to categorize potential causes of a problem, used to identify its root cause.

Access Management

Access Management is critical part of IT Service Management (ITSM), responsible to manage and control the user access for systems and IT resources. Primary goal is to ensure the user access are appropriate for respective resources and well within security compliance.

1. Initiating Access Requests

- **Request Submission Process:** Users submit requests for access to IT resources, such as systems, applications, or data, through a defined procedure.
- **Validating Request:** Each request go through validation to confirm the user's legitimate need for access and to validate the authenticity of the request.

2. Approval of Access

- **Authorization Review:** Authorized personnel, including managers, system owners, or security officers, review and approve access requests based on predefined criteria and process.
- **Compliance Assurance:** Each request is evaluated to ensure it aligns with the organization's security policies and regulatory standards.

3. Provisioning of Access

- **Access Implementation:** Once approved, the user is granted the necessary access rights, with permissions, roles, or credentials configured as needed.

- **System Updates:** All relevant systems and databases are updated to reflect the new access permissions, ensuring accurate records are maintained.

4. Ongoing Access Management

- **Role-Based Access Control (RBAC):** Access is managed using predefined roles that come with specific permissions, allowing for efficient and consistent access control.

- **Least Privilege Principle:** Access rights are restricted to the minimum level necessary for users to perform their roles, thereby reducing security risks.

- **Regular Access Reviews:** Periodic reviews are conducted to ensure that users' access rights remain appropriate as their roles and responsibilities change.

5. Access Monitoring

- **Logging Activities:** Access-related activities, including logins and permission changes, are logged for auditing and monitoring purposes.

- **Detecting Inconsistencies:** Monitoring systems are in place to detect unusual or unauthorized access patterns, triggering alerts and investigations as needed.

6. Revoking Access

- **Deactivation of Access:** When access is no longer required, such as when an employee leaves or changes roles, their access rights are promptly revoked or deactivated.

- **Access Elimination:** Regular audits are conducted to remove obsolete or unused access permissions, maintaining a secure environment.

7. Conducting Access Audits

- **Periodic Audits:** Regular audits of access rights are performed to ensure ongoing compliance with security policies and regulatory requirements.

- **Access Certification:** Managers and system owners periodically review and certify that all existing access rights are necessary and appropriate.

8. Documentation and Reporting

- **Record Keeping:** Comprehensive records of all access-related activities, including requests, approvals, and revocations, are maintained for auditing purposes.

- **Activity Reporting:** Regular reports are generated to provide insights into access management activities, including compliance checks, access reviews, and incidents.

9. Continuous Improvement in Access Management

- **Process Optimization:** The access management process is continually reviewed and refined to enhance efficiency, security, and compliance.

- **Training Programs:** Ongoing training and awareness initiatives are provided to keep users and administrators informed about the latest access management policies and best practices.

Benefits of Effective Access Management

- **Increased Security:** By ensuring that only authorized individuals can access sensitive resources, the risk of data breaches and unauthorized access is minimized.

- **Regulatory Compliance:** Access Management helps organizations meet regulatory requirements and adhere to internal policies concerning data protection and access control.

- **Operational Efficiency:** Streamlined processes for managing and granting access reduce administrative burdens and improve response times.

- **Enhanced Productivity:** Users are granted timely access to the resources they need, allowing them to perform their duties effectively.

- **Audit Trail:** A well-maintained audit trail of access-related activities supports compliance audits and investigations.

Best Practices and Techniques in Access Management

- **Single Sign-On (SSO):** SSO simplifies access by allowing users to log in to multiple systems using a single set of credentials.

- **Multi-Factor Authentication (MFA):** MFA enhances security by requiring users to verify their identity through multiple methods before gaining access.

- **Access Control Lists (ACLs):** ACLs define and manage user permissions for specific resources, ensuring that only authorized users have the necessary access.

- **Identity and Access Management (IAM) Tools:** Specialized IAM tools are used to automate and streamline access control processes, improving both efficiency and security.

Essential Service Desk Metrics and KPIs

To maintain high performance and operational excellence, service desks must track specific metrics and Key Performance Indicators (KPIs). These metrics provide crucial insights into the service desk's effectiveness, pinpoint areas needing attention, and ensure alignment with the organization's strategic goals. Below are key metrics and KPIs to consider:

1. Response Time

- **What It Measures**: The average duration it takes for the service desk to respond to an initial user request.

- **Why It Matters**: A quick response demonstrates efficiency and responsiveness, leading to increased user satisfaction.

2. Resolution Time

- **What It Measures**: The average time required to fully resolve an incident from when it is first reported.

- **Why It Matters**: Faster resolution enhances user productivity by minimizing downtime, contributing to a better overall experience.

3. Incident Volume

- **What It Measures**: The total number of incidents reported to the service desk over a specified time frame.

- **Why It Matters**: Understanding incident trends helps in identifying recurring issues and implementing preventive strategies to reduce future incidents.

4. SLA Compliance

- **What It Measures**: The percentage of incidents resolved within the agreed-upon Service Level Agreement (SLA) timelines.

- **Why It Matters**: Meeting SLAs is crucial for maintaining user trust and ensuring the service desk fulfills its obligations to the organization.

5. User Satisfaction (CSAT)

- **What It Measures**: The level of satisfaction users have with the service desk, typically assessed through surveys after issue resolution.

- **Why It Matters**: High satisfaction scores indicate effective service delivery, while low scores highlight areas that may need improvement.

6. Ticket Backlog

- **What It Measures**: The number of unresolved tickets at any given moment.

- **Why It Matters**: A large or growing backlog may signal inefficiencies or resource shortages, necessitating immediate attention to maintain service quality.

7. Incident Reopen Rate

- **What It Measures**: The percentage of incidents that are reopened after being marked as resolved.

- **Why It Matters**: A high reopen rate suggests that initial resolutions may have been inadequate, requiring further investigation into recurring issues or resolution quality.

8. Agent Utilization Rate

- **What It Measures**: The proportion of time service desk agents spend on productive tasks versus idle time.

- **Why It Matters**: High utilization indicates that resources are being used effectively, while low utilization could reveal opportunities for optimizing workflows.

9. First-Level Resolution Rate

- **What It Measures**: The percentage of incidents resolved by the first level of support without needing to escalate to higher tiers.

- **Why It Matters**: A high first-level resolution rate shows the competence of frontline support, reducing the need for escalations and speeding up the resolution process.

10. Mean Time to Acknowledge (MTTA)

- **What It Measures**: The average time taken for the service desk to acknowledge an incident after it has been reported.

- **Why It Matters**: Prompt acknowledgment reassures users that their issues are being prioritized and addressed, even before resolution begins.

11. Mean Time to Resolve (MTTR)

- **What It Measures**: The average time taken to resolve an incident from the time it was first logged.

- **Why It Matters**: A lower MTTR is indicative of a highly efficient service desk, which minimizes disruption and ensures quick restoration of services.

12. Knowledge Base Utilization

- **What It Measures**: The frequency and effectiveness of the knowledge base's use by both users and service desk agents.

- **Why It Matters**: A well-utilized knowledge base facilitates self-service and quicker problem resolution, reducing the overall workload on the service desk.

13. Training and Certification Levels

- **What It Measures**: The percentage of service desk agents who have completed relevant training and earned certifications.

- **Why It Matters**: Ensuring agents are well-trained and certified enhances their ability to resolve incidents effectively, leading to better service outcomes.

Benefits of Monitoring Service Desk Metrics and KPIs

By consistently tracking and analyzing service desk metrics and KPIs, organizations can reap several benefits:

- **Enhanced Performance**: Metrics highlight areas that need improvement, driving continuous enhancement of service desk operations.

- **Data-Driven Decisions**: KPIs provide objective data that informs strategic decisions and resource allocation.

- **Higher User Satisfaction**: Consistently meeting or exceeding service expectations ensures users remain satisfied and confident in the service desk's capabilities.

- **Proactive Issue Management**: Early detection of potential issues allows for preemptive actions, preventing problems from escalating.

- **Clear Accountability**: Establishing KPIs sets clear expectations and accountability, ensuring that service desk staff are aligned with performance goals.

Best Practices for Implementing Service Desk Metrics and KPIs

To effectively implement and take the benefit from service desk metrics and KPIs, consider these best practices:

- **Align with Organizational Objectives**: Ensure that the selected metrics and KPIs support and cover the broader goals and priorities of your organization.

- **Continuous Monitoring and Analysis**: Regularly review and analyze your metrics to identify trends, assess performance, and identify areas for improvement.

- **Translate Data into Action**: Use insights derived from KPIs to drive improvements in service desk operations and make informed decisions.

- **Incorporate User Feedback**: Actively seek and integrate user feedback into performance evaluations to ensure the service desk is meeting user expectations.

- **Invest in Ongoing Training**: Provide continual training and certification opportunities for service desk agents, informed by performance data and identified skill gaps.

Assessing Success and Improving Service Desk Metrics and KPIs

Effectively assessing success and driving improvement in service desk metrics and KPIs requires a systematic methodical approach that focuses on data collection, thorough analysis, and strategic actions. Below are the best practices can be adapted to assess and improve.

1. Define & Set Clear and Aligned Goals

- **Business Alignment**: Make sure that your service desk metrics and KPIs are directly associated to your organization's broader objectives.

- **SMART Goal Setting**: Develop goals that are Specific, Measurable, Achievable, Relevant, and Time-bound for each metric to provide clear direction and success criteria.

2. Data Baseline and Compare Industry Standards

- **Current Performance Levels**: Identify your existing performance levels for each metric to create a baseline for future improvements.

- **Industry Standards**: Compare your metrics with industry standard benchmarks to identify areas where your service desk may be falling short or excelling.

3. Ongoing Monitoring and Reporting

- **Continuous Monitoring**: Utilize real-time dashboards and monitoring tools to keep a close eye on key performance metrics.

- **Routine Reporting**: Regularly generate and share reports—whether daily, weekly, or monthly—to track performance trends and identify any deviations from expected targets.

4. Data Analysis and Trend Identification

- **Identify Patterns**: Analyze historical data to identify patterns, trends, and recurring issues that may need to be addressed.

- **Root Cause Analysis**: Perform root cause analysis on significant deviations from targets to uncover the root of the problem.

5. Implement a Continuous Improvement Process

- **Adopt the PDCA Cycle**: Use the Plan-Do-Check-Act cycle to continuously refine and enhance service desk operations:

  - **Plan**: Identify areas needing improvement and create detailed action plans.

  - **Do**: Implement the proposed changes or improvements.

  - **Check**: Monitor the outcomes to assess the effectiveness of the changes.

- ○ **Act**: Standardize successful changes and make necessary adjustments to those that didn't meet expectations.

- **Create Feedback Mechanisms**: Set up a continuous feedback loop to gather ongoing input from both users and staff, enabling ongoing refinement.

6. Effectively Leverage KPIs

- **Prioritize Impactful Metrics**: Focus on KPIs that directly impact and influence user satisfaction, operational efficiency, and overall business performance.

- **Balanced Measurement Approach**: Apply a balanced scorecard to evaluate performance across various dimensions, such as financial health, customer satisfaction, internal processes, and employee development.

7. Advanced Tools and Technology Usage

- **Implement ITSM Tools**: Implement IT service management solutions to automate data collection, monitoring, and reporting.

- **Leverage Analytics**: Leverage advanced analytics platforms to gain deeper insights into service desk performance and user behavior.

8. Staff Development and Empowerment

- **Ongoing Skill Development**: Provide continuous training opportunities to enhance the skills, experience, and knowledge of your service desk team.

- **Encourage Ownership**: Empower staff to take responsibility for their performance and actively contribute ideas to improve the processes.

9. Stakeholders Engagement

- **User Insights Collection**: Regularly collect feedback from users through surveys, interviews, and focus groups to understand their satisfaction levels and needs.

- **Collaborate with Stakeholders**: Engage key stakeholders in setting performance targets and reviewing results to make sure they are aligned with organizational goals.

10. Recognize Achievements and Celebrate Success

- **Success Criteria Definition**: Clearly define what success looks like for each metric and regularly assess progress against these criteria.

- **Celebrate and Reward**: Acknowledge and reward employees for meeting performance targets and contributing to process and service improvements.

Key Metrics and KPIs to Focus On:

First Contact Resolution (FCR): This metric assesses the percentage of incidents resolved during the initial interaction. A high FCR indicates that the service desk is effective in addressing issues promptly, reducing the need for follow-up interactions and enhancing user satisfaction.

Average Response Time: This KPI measures the speed at which the service desk acknowledges user requests. A shorter response time reflects the desk's attentiveness and readiness to assist users, which is crucial for maintaining user trust and satisfaction.

Average Resolution Time: This metric tracks the average time taken to resolve incidents. It provides insights into the efficiency of the resolution process, helping to identify areas where the process can be streamlined to reduce downtime and improve user experience.

Customer Satisfaction (CSAT): Captured through surveys, this metric provides direct feedback from users about their experience with the service desk. High CSAT scores indicate that the service desk is meeting or exceeding user expectations, which is vital for maintaining a positive reputation.

Net Promoter Score (NPS): This indicator measures how likely users are to recommend the service desk to others. A high NPS suggests strong user loyalty and satisfaction, while a low NPS can highlight areas needing improvement.

Ticket Volume: This metric counts the number of tickets received by the service desk. Analyzing ticket volume helps in understanding workload trends, identifying peak times, and recognizing recurring issues that may need a more permanent solution.

Backlog of Open Tickets: By monitoring the number of open tickets, this KPI highlights potential bottlenecks in the resolution process. A growing backlog can indicate resource constraints or inefficiencies that need to be addressed to maintain service quality.

Mean Time to Recovery (MTTR): This measures the average time required to restore service after an incident. Minimizing MTTR is crucial for reducing service disruptions and maintaining operational continuity.

Cost per Ticket: This metric analyzes the cost associated with resolving each incident. Understanding cost per ticket helps in budget management and identifying opportunities for cost-efficiency improvements without compromising service quality.

Agent Utilization: By tracking the productivity and workload of service desk agents, this KPI ensures that resources are allocated effectively. High agent utilization indicates that the team is working efficiently, while low utilization may suggest underuse of resources.

Escalation Rate: This tracks the percentage of incidents that require escalation to higher support levels. A high escalation rate can indicate complex issues or gaps in frontline support that need to be addressed through training or process improvements.

Adherence to SLAs (Service Level Agreements): This measures the service desk's compliance with agreed-upon service levels. Adhering to SLAs is essential for meeting user expectations and maintaining contractual obligations.

Framework for continuous improvement

1. *Current Performance Evaluation.*

- **Performance Metrics Review:** Analyze current KPIs such as First Contact Resolution (FCR), Average Response

Time, Customer Satisfaction (CSAT), and Net Promoter Score (NPS) to gauge current performance.

- **User Feedback Collection:** Collect and assess feedback from users to pinpoint common issues and areas for improvement.

- **Industry Benchmarking:** Compare your service desk's performance with industry standards bench marks to identify gaps and improvement opportunities.

2. Set Clear Objectives

- **Define Improvement Goals:** Establish specific, measurable goals based on the assessment. For instance, aim to reduce Average Response Time by 20% or boost CSAT scores by 10%.

- **Prioritize Initiatives:** Identify and prioritize initiatives that will most effectively achieve these goals.

3. Optimize Processes

- **Workflow Reviews:** Review and refine service desk operational workflows to eliminate inefficiencies and improve overall efficiency.

- **Implement Automation:** Identify and Implement automation for repetitive tasks to allow agents to focus on more complex issues.

- **Enhance Knowledge Management:** Develop a robust knowledge base to facilitate quicker resolution of common problems.

4. Invest on Training and Development

- **Assess Skills:** Review the current skill levels of service desk agents to identify training requirement.

- **Develop Training Programs:** Design and implement training programs to improve technical skills, customer service capabilities, and familiarity with new tools and processes.

- **Continuous Learning Encouragement:** Foster a culture of continuous learning through regular workshops and certifications.

5. Upgrade Technology and Tools

- **Current Tools Assessment:** Assess the effectiveness of current tools and technologies used by the service desk.

- **Invest in Modern Solutions:** Implement and adapt modern service desk software with features like ticket management, reporting, and analytics.

- **Ensure Smooth Integration:** New tools integration with existing systems to maintain smooth operations.

6. Monitor and Report Progress

- **Real-Time Monitoring:** Implement and adapt real-time monitoring of key metrics to quickly identify and address issues.

- **Regular Reporting:** Establish a regular reporting schedules to analyze and track progress against goals and make data-driven decisions.

- **Create Feedback Loops:** Develop feedback loops with users and agents to continuously gather insights and make improvements.

7. Engage with Users

- **Communicate Changes:** Keep users informed about changes and improvements to the service desk through regular updates.

- **Involve Users:** Engage users in the improvement process by seeking their input and feedback on proposed changes.

- **Conduct Satisfaction Surveys:** Regularly conduct satisfaction surveys to gauge user sentiment and identify areas for further improvement.

8. Commit to Continuous Improvement

- **Review and Adjust:** Regularly review the improvement plan and adjust strategies based on performance data and feedback.

- **Encourage Innovation:** Foster innovation and experimentation with new ideas and technologies to stay ahead of industry trends.

- **Recognize Contributions:** Acknowledge and reward agents and teams that contribute to the success of improvement initiatives.

Chapter Summary – Mindmap

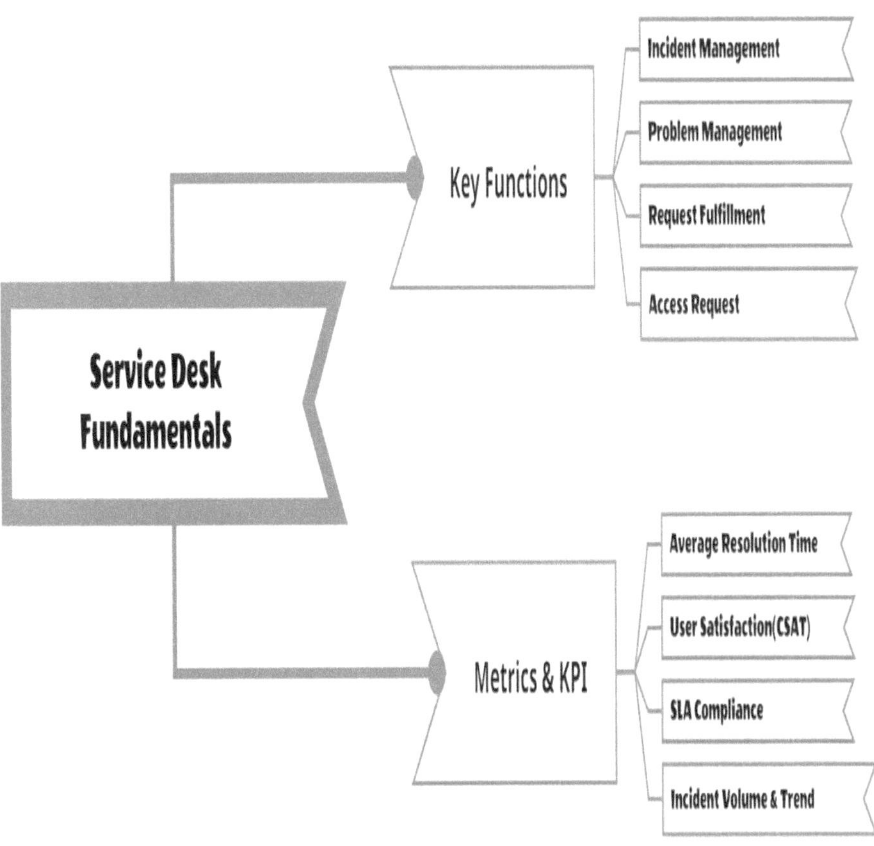

Chapter 3

Setting Up a Service Desk

Setting up a service desk consist of detailed steps and various considerations to effectively support users and customers while aligning with the organization's goals. Below are the comprehensive steps to follow when establishing a service desk.

1. Define Scope and Objective

- **Objectives:** Clearly define the objective and what you want to achieve with the service desk (e.g., reduce downtime, enhance support efficiency, improve user satisfaction, support 24X7 customers).

- **Scope:** Clearly identify the scope of services the service desk will offer (e.g., IT support, customer service, internal employee support).

2. Identify Stakeholders

- **Key Stakeholders:** key stakeholders' identification, including management, IT staff, end-users, and any external vendors and partners.

- **Stakeholder Engagement:** Work with stakeholders to plan and gather requirements, expectations, and feedback.

3. Choose a Service Desk Model

- **Outsourced Vs. In-House:** Decide whether the service desk team will be managed internally in-house or outsourced to a third-party service provider.

- **Centralized vs. Decentralized:** Choose between a centralized service desk (one location) or decentralized (multiple locations or teams).

4. Right Technology Selection

- **Service Desk Software:** Choosing comprehensive IT service management (ITSM) tool that supports ticketing, tracking, reporting, and automation.

- **Integration:** Make sure the service desk software integrates with existing systems (e.g., monitoring tools).

5. Service Desk Processes Design

- **Incident Management:** Define processes for logging, categorizing, prioritizing, and resolving incidents.

- **Request Fulfillment:** Define procedures for handling service requests, such as access requests or any other request.

- **Problem Management:** Define the processes for identifying and addressing recurring issues.

- **Change Management:** Define the process for managing changes to IT services and infrastructure.

- **Knowledge Management:** Outline the process and develop documentation, including solutions, FAQs, and best practices.

6. Define Roles and Responsibilities

- **Staffing:** Determine the staffing requirements, including the number of agents, supervisors, and managers.

- **Roles:** Define clear roles and responsibilities for each team member (e.g., first-level support, second-level support, Service Desk Lead, service desk manager).

- **Skills, Experience and Training:** Ensure staff have the necessary skills, experience, and provide ongoing training and development.

7. Define Service Level Agreements (SLAs)

- **SLAs:** Define SLAs for response and resolution times for different types of incidents and service requests.

- **Performance Metrics:** Set up key performance indicators (KPIs) to measure compliance with SLAs and overall service desk performance.

8. Set Up Communication Channels

- **Multichannel Support:** Provide multiple channels for users to contact the service desk (e.g., phone, email, web portal, chat).

- **Self-Service:** Create self-service options, such as a knowledge base or automated chatbots, to empower users to resolve issues independently.

9. Develop a Service Catalog

- **Services Offered:** Define a service catalog that lists all the services offered by the service desk, including descriptions and how to request them.

- **Visibility and Access:** Ensure service catalog easily accessible to users through the web portal or intranet.

10. Implement Monitoring and Reporting

- **Real-Time Monitoring:** Set up real-time monitoring to track incidents, requests, and service desk activities.

- **Reporting:** Generate regular reports on KPI's and Key metrics to analyze trend, performance and identify areas for improvement.

11. Launch and Promote the Service Desk

- **Communication Plan:** Design a good communication plan to inform users about the service desk, its services, and share the contact details.

- **Training and Onboarding:** Provide training sessions and onboarding materials for new users to familiarize them with the service desk processes.

12. Continuous Improvement

- **Feedback Loop:** Establish a feedback loop to gather user and customer feedback and make continuous improvements to service desk operations.

- **Review and Refine:** Regularly review service desk performance, processes, and tools, and refine them based on feedback and performance data.

3.1 Building a Service Desk Team

Building an effective service desk team involves careful planning, selection, training, and continuous development. Follow the below steps to build a strong service desk team:

1. Define Team Structure and Roles

- **Team Structure:** Define the structure of the service desk team, considering factors like size, scope of services, and user and customer base.

- **Roles and Responsibilities:**

  - **Service Desk Manager:** Oversees the entire service desk operation, define goals, and ensures organizational objectives are met.

  - **Team Leaders/Supervisors:** Managing day-to-day operations, provide guidance, and handling escalations.

  - **First-Level Support:** Handles initial user interactions, resolves basic issues, and escalates more complex issues or requests.

  - **Second-Level Support:** Resolve more complex issues that require specialized knowledge and experience.

  - **Subject Matter Experts (SMEs):** Provides expertise in specific areas, such as software applications, infrastructure, etc.

  - **Knowledge Managers:** Manage the knowledge base and make sure it is up-to-date and useful.

  - **Incident and Problem Managers:** Responsible to manage incidents and problems.

2. Hiring the Right People

- **Job Descriptions:** Create detailed job descriptions for each role, outlining required skills, qualifications, experience, and responsibilities.

- **Recruitment Channels:** Work with recruitment channels, such as job boards, social media, and professional networks, to attract qualified and competent candidates.

- **Interview Process:** Develop a structured interview process to assess technical skills, problem-solving abilities, communication skills, attitude and cultural fit.

- **Assessment Tests:** Practical exercises and tests can be used to evaluate candidates' technical knowledge, experience and problem-solving skill and ability.

3. Onboarding and Training

- **Comprehensive Onboarding:** Design and establish a thorough onboarding process to help new hires understand the organization culture, service desk processes, tools, and expectations.

- **Initial Training:** Offer initial training on technical skills, customer service, incident management, and any specific software or tools used.

- **Ongoing Training:** Provide continuous training opportunities to keep team members updated on new technologies, processes, and best practices.

4. Establish a Positive Team Culture

- **Collaboration:** Encourage a collaborative environment where team members can share knowledge, ideas and support each other.

- **Communication:** Establish and encourage open and transparent communication styles within the team and with other departments.

- **Recognition and Rewards:** Regularly recognize and reward team members for their contributions and achievements to motivate and boost their morale.

- **Team Building:** Organize regular team-building activities to strengthen relationships and understanding. Eg. Team lunch and outings to develop a good bonding within the team.

5. Set Clear Goals and Expectations

- **Performance Goals:** Set clear, achievable performance goals for the team and individual members.

- **Expectations:** Communicate expectations regarding performance, behavior, and customer service standards.

- **KPIs:** Define and establish key performance indicators (KPIs) to measure individual and team performance, such as, average response time, average resolution time and user satisfaction.

6. Provide the Right Tools and Resources

- **Service Desk Software:** Enable the team with comprehensive service desk software that supports ticketing, tracking, reporting, and knowledge management.

- **Knowledge Base:** Maintain an up-to-date knowledge base to help team members resolve issues quickly and efficiently.

- **Remote Support Tools:** Provide remote support tools to assist remote users.

- **Training Materials:** Make sure team has access to training materials, documentation, and other resources that team can refer for learn & grow.

7. Implement Effective Processes

- **Standard Operating Procedures (SOPs):** Define and document SOPs for common service desk day to day operations and processes.

- **Escalation Procedures:** Establish clear escalation procedures for handling critical or high-priority issues.

- **Quality Assurance:** Implement quality assurance processes to monitor and improve service desk performance and customer interactions.

8. Monitor and Review Performance

- **Regular Reviews:** Conduct regular performance reviews to provide feedback, set new goals, and identify improvement areas.

- **Metrics and Reporting:** Use service desk KPIs and key metrics to monitor performance, identify trends, and make appropriate decisions based on data analysis.

- **User Feedback:** Collect and analyze user feedback to understand their needs and satisfaction levels, and to identify improvement opportunities.

9. Continuous Improvement

- **Feedback Loop:** Establish a feedback loop to gather input from team members and users for ongoing improvements.

- **Process Optimization:** Regularly review and optimize service desk processes to enhance efficiency and effectiveness.

- **Professional Development:** Support professional development by offering training, certifications, and career advancement opportunities.

10. Adapt to Changing Needs

- **Scalability:** Ensure the service desk team can scale to meet growing demands as the organization expands.

- **Flexibility:** Be flexible and adaptable to changing technologies, processes, and user needs.

- **Innovation:** Encourage innovation and the adoption of new tools and methods to improve service desk operations.

3.1.1 Roles and Responsibilities

In a service desk team, each role has specific responsibilities to ensure efficient and effective support. Below are the breakdown of the key roles and their responsibilities:

1. Service Desk Manager

- **Leadership:** Lead and manage the service desk team, setting goals, and ensuring alignment with organizational objectives.

- **Strategy:** Develop and implement service desk strategies and policies.

- **Performance Management:** Monitor team performance, set KPIs, and ensure SLA compliance.

- **Continuous Improvement:** Identify areas for process improvement and implement changes.
- **Stakeholder Communication:** Communicate with key stakeholders to understand their needs and report on service desk performance.
- **Budgeting:** Manage the service desk budget, including staffing, tools, and training.

2. Team Leaders/Supervisors

- **Day-to-Day Operations Management:** Oversee daily operations, ensuring smooth functioning of the service desk.
- **Support and Guidance:** Provide support, guidance, and training to service desk analysts.
- **Escalation Handling:** Handle escalated issues that first-level support cannot resolve.
- **Performance Monitoring:** Monitor team performance and ensure adherence to SLAs and KPIs.
- **Reporting:** Prepare and present performance reports to the service desk manager.

3.Service Desk Analysts

- **Initial Contact:** Act as the first point of contact for users, handling incoming calls, emails, and chat requests.
- **Issue Resolution:** Resolve basic technical issues, service requests, and provide general assistance.
- **Ticket Logging:** Log and categorize incidents and service requests in the ticketing system.

- **Escalation:** Escalate complex issues to second-level support or specialized teams on need basis.

- **Customer Service:** Provide excellent customer service and ensure a positive user experience.

4. Subject Matter Experts (SMEs)

- **Specialized Support:** Provide expertise in specific areas, such as infra issues, software applications, etc.

- **Advanced Troubleshooting:** Assist second-level support with advanced troubleshooting and problem resolution.

- **Knowledge Sharing:** Share knowledge and provide training to other team members.

5. Knowledge Managers

- **Knowledge Base Maintenance:** Maintain and update the service desk knowledge base and keep it up to date.

- **Content Creation:** Create and share knowledge articles, FAQs, and troubleshooting guides.

- **Training:** Provide training to service desk agents on new knowledge articles and best practices.

- **Quality Assurance:** Ensure the accuracy and relevance of knowledge base content.

6. Incident Managers

- **Incident Handling:** Oversee the incident management process, ensuring timely resolution of incidents.

- **Coordination:** Coordinate with different teams and stakeholders to resolve incidents.

- **Reporting:** Monitor incident trends and report on incident management performance.

- **Process Improvement:** Identify and implement improvements to the incident management process.

7. Problem Managers

- **Problem Identification:** Identify recurring incidents and underlying problems.

- **Root Cause Analysis:** Conduct root cause analysis to determine the cause of problems.

- **Permanent Solutions:** Develop and implement permanent solutions to prevent recurrence of incidents or issues.

- **Documentation:** Document problems and solutions in the problem management database.

3.1.2 Skills and Competencies Required for IT service desk team.

An IT service desk team requires a blend of technical skills, interpersonal competencies, and problem-solving abilities to effectively support users and manage IT services. Here are the key skills and competencies necessary for an IT service desk team:

1. Technical Skills

- **Basic IT Knowledge:** Understanding of fundamental IT concepts, hardware, software, and networking.

- **Operating Systems:** Proficiency in using and troubleshooting various operating systems (Windows, macOS, Linux).

- **Software Applications:** Knowledge of common software applications, including office suites, email clients, and collaboration tools.

- **Network Fundamentals:** Understanding of network basics, including IP addressing, DNS, DHCP, and common network issues.

- **Remote Support Tools:** Familiarity with remote support tools and techniques for diagnosing and resolving issues.

- **ITSM Tools:** Proficiency in using IT service management (ITSM) tools for ticketing, tracking, and reporting.

2. Interpersonal Skills

- **Communication:** Excellent verbal and written communication skills to interact effectively with users and team members.

- **Active Listening:** Ability to listen actively to understand user issues and concerns accurately.

- **Empathy:** Demonstrating empathy and understanding towards users' problems and frustrations.

- **Patience:** Remaining patient and calm, especially when dealing with frustrated or non-technical users.

- **Team Collaboration:** Ability to work well within a team, sharing knowledge and supporting colleagues.

3. Problem-Solving Skills

- **Analytical Thinking:** Ability to analyze problems, identify root causes, and develop effective solutions.

- **Troubleshooting**: Strong troubleshooting skills to diagnose and resolve technical issues efficiently.

- **Attention to Detail**: Paying attention to details to ensure accurate problem resolution and documentation.

- **Critical Thinking**: Applying critical thinking to evaluate different solutions and choose the most effective one.

4. Customer Service Skills

- **User-Focused**: Putting the customers first and ensuring a positive customer or user experience.

- **Service Orientation**: Commitment to providing high-quality service and meeting customer needs.

- **Conflict Resolution**: Handling difficult situations and conflicts with customers professionally and effectively.

- **Time Management**: Managing time effectively to handle multiple requests and meet response/resolution times.

5. Organizational Skills

- **Prioritization**: Ability to prioritize tasks and incidents based on urgency and impact.

- **Documentation**: Maintaining accurate and detailed documentation of incidents, requests, and resolutions.

- **Follow-Up**: Ensuring follow-up on unresolved issues and keeping users informed of progress.

- **Multitasking**: Managing multiple tasks and incidents simultaneously without compromising quality.

6. Adaptability and Learning

- **Flexibility:** Adapting to changing technologies, processes, time zones and user needs.

- **Continuous Learning:** Commitment to continuous learning and staying updated with the latest IT trends and best practices.

- **Problem Anticipation:** Ability to anticipate potential issues and proactively address them.

7. Technical Certification and Training

- **ITIL Certification:** Knowledge of ITIL (Information Technology Infrastructure Library) practices and certification can be beneficial.

- **Specific Tools Training:** Training in specific tools and platforms used by the organization (e.g., ServiceNow, Service Cloud, Jira).

8. Process and Policy Knowledge

- **IT Policies:** Understanding of the organization's IT policies and procedures.

- **Compliance:** Knowledge of compliance requirements related to data security, privacy, and regulatory standards.

- **Incident Management:** Familiarity with incident management processes and best practices.

- **Change Management:** Understanding of change management processes and their impact on IT services.

9. Soft Skills

- **Positive Attitude:** Maintaining a positive and constructive attitude, especially under pressure.

- **Dependability:** Being reliable and consistent in performance and attendance.

- **Professionalism:** Demonstrating professionalism in interactions and communication.

- **Initiative:** Taking initiative to identify and address issues proactively.

10. Leadership Skills (for Managers and Supervisors)

- **Team Leadership:** Ability to lead, motivate, and manage a team effectively.

- **Decision-Making:** Making informed decisions that align with organizational goals and service desk objectives.

- **Conflict Management:** Handling conflicts within the team and resolving them constructively.

- **Performance Management:** Monitoring and evaluating team performance, providing feedback, and facilitating growth.

3.2 Service Desk Tools and Technologies for IT infrastructure

Implementing the right tools and technologies is crucial for the effective functioning of an IT service desk. Here are some essential service desk tools and technologies that can help streamline processes, improve efficiency, and enhance user satisfaction:

1. Ticketing and Incident Management Systems

- **ServiceNow:** A comprehensive ITSM tool that offers ticketing, incident management, change management, and asset management.

- **Jira Service Management:** A flexible and powerful service desk tool from Atlassian that integrates well with Jira Software for development teams.

- **Zendesk:** A popular support tool that offers ticketing, automation, and reporting features tailored for both IT and customer service.

- **Freshservice:** An intuitive and easy-to-use ITSM tool with robust ticketing, asset management, and change management capabilities.

- **Service Cloud:** Oracle Service Cloud, also known as Oracle RightNow, is a robust customer service and support platform that includes a comprehensive ticketing system.

2. Remote Support Tools

- **TeamViewer:** A widely used remote support tool that allows IT staff to remotely access and control user devices to resolve issues.

- **AnyDesk:** A lightweight and fast remote desktop tool for providing remote support and troubleshooting.

- **LogMeIn Rescue:** A powerful remote support tool designed for IT professionals, offering remote access, diagnostics, and troubleshooting features.

- **Microsoft Remote Desktop:** A built-in tool for Windows environments that provides remote access and support capabilities.

3. Knowledge Management Systems

- **Confluence:** A knowledge management tool from Atlassian that allows teams to create, share, and manage knowledge base articles and documentation.

- **SharePoint:** A Microsoft platform for creating internal knowledge bases, document libraries, and collaborative spaces.

- **Guru:** A knowledge management solution that integrates with other tools to provide in-context knowledge to support agents.

4. Monitoring and Alerting Tools

- **Nagios:** An open-source monitoring tool that provides comprehensive monitoring and alerting for servers, network devices, and applications.

- **Zabbix:** Another open-source monitoring solution that offers real-time monitoring and performance tracking of IT infrastructure.

- **SolarWinds:** A suite of monitoring and management tools for network performance, server health, and application monitoring.

- **Datadog:** A cloud-based monitoring and analytics platform for infrastructure, applications, logs, and more.

5. Communication and Collaboration Tools

- **Slack:** A popular team communication tool that integrates with various service desk and monitoring tools to provide real-time updates and collaboration.

- **Microsoft Teams:** A collaboration platform that integrates with Office 365 and offers chat, video conferencing, and integration with other IT tools.

- **Zoom:** A widely used video conferencing tool that can be used for remote support sessions and team meetings.

- **Google Workspace:** A suite of productivity and collaboration tools including Gmail, Google Drive, and Google Meet.

6. Self-Service Portals and Chatbots

- **ServiceNow Virtual Agent:** An AI-powered chatbot that can handle common user requests and provide self-service options.

- **Zendesk Guide:** A self-service portal that allows users to find answers and solutions through a knowledge base and community forums.

- **Freshservice Self-Service Portal:** A customizable portal for users to submit tickets, access knowledge base articles, and track ticket status.

8. Change Management Tools

- **BMC Remedy:** A powerful ITSM suite that includes change management, incident management, and problem management.

- **Cherwell Service Management:** A flexible and customizable ITSM tool with comprehensive change management capabilities.

- **Ivanti Service Manager:** An ITSM solution that supports change management, incident management, and other ITIL processes.

3.2.1 Ticketing Systems

Ticketing systems are essential tools for IT service desks to manage, track, and resolve user requests and issues efficiently. Here are some of the most widely used ticketing systems, along with their key features:

1. ServiceNow

- **Overview:** A comprehensive IT service management (ITSM) tool that offers extensive features for ticketing, incident management, change management, and asset management.

- **Key Features:**
  - Customizable workflows and automation
  - Integration with other IT and business systems
  - Self-service portal and knowledge base
  - Advanced reporting and analytics
  - Mobile app for remote access

2. Jira Service Management

- **Overview:** A flexible and powerful service desk tool from Atlassian that integrates well with Jira Software, making it ideal for development and IT operations teams.

- **Key Features:**

    - Configurable workflows and automation

    - Incident, problem, and change management.

    - SLA management and reporting

    - Knowledge base integration with Confluence

    - Real-time collaboration with team members

3. Zendesk

- **Overview:** A popular customer service and support tool that offers robust ticketing, automation, and reporting features tailored for both IT and customer service environments.

- **Key Features:**

    - Multichannel support (email, chat, phone, social media)

    - Customizable ticket fields and workflows

    - Self-service portal and community forums

    - AI-powered chatbot for automated responses

    - Comprehensive analytics and reporting

4. Freshservice

- **Overview:** An intuitive and easy-to-use ITSM tool from Freshworks that provides robust ticketing, asset management, and change management capabilities.

- **Key Features:**

    - Automation for repetitive tasks and workflows

- Incident, problem, change, and release management
- Asset and configuration management
- Self-service portal and knowledge base
- Advanced analytics and reporting

5. Service Cloud: Oracle Service Cloud, also known as Oracle RightNow, is a robust customer service and support platform that includes a comprehensive ticketing system.

- **Key Features:**
  - Multi-channel support (email, chat, social media, phone).
  - Knowledge management for self-service.
  - Incident and case management.
  - Advanced analytics and reporting.
  - Automation and workflow capabilities.
  - Customer feedback and survey tools.

Chapter Summary – Mindmap

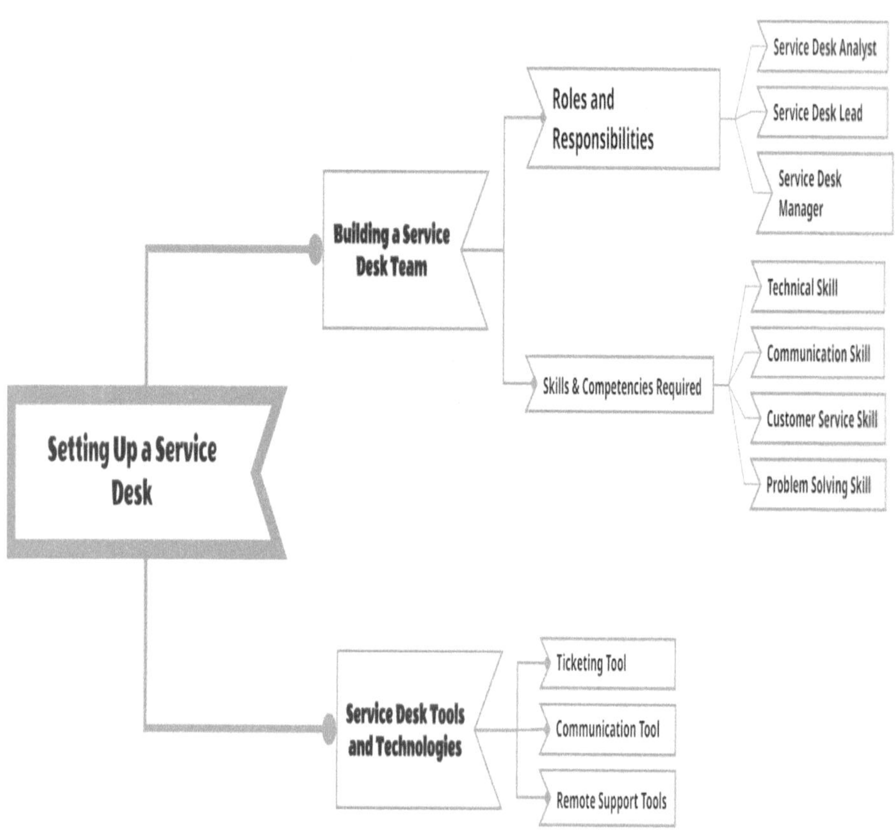

Chapter 4

Service Desk Processes and Best Practices

Service desk processes and best practices are essential for efficient IT support and customer satisfaction.

Key processes include incident management, request fulfillment, problem management, and change management.

Best practices involve implementing a standardized workflow, utilizing a robust ticketing system, and ensuring clear communication channels.

Regular training for staff, proactive problem-solving, and continuous improvement through feedback and metrics analysis are crucial.

Prioritizing customer experience, maintaining a knowledge base, and adhering to ITIL (Information Technology Infrastructure Library) guidelines can significantly enhance service desk operations.

These practices ensure timely resolution of issues, minimize disruptions, and improve overall service quality.

1. ITIL Framework Overview

What is ITIL?

- **ITIL Definition:** ITIL is a framework of best practices designed to align IT services with the needs of the business. It provides a structured approach to IT service management, focusing on delivering value and maintaining stability in the IT environment.

Key Concepts of ITIL:

1. **Service:** ITIL views IT services as the means of delivering value to customers by facilitating outcomes, customers want to achieve without the ownership of specific costs and risks.

2. **Service Management:** The practice of managing IT services throughout their lifecycle, from inception through development and deployment, to ongoing support and improvement.

3. **IT Service Lifecycle:** ITIL organizes IT services into a lifecycle composed of five stages:

   - **Service Strategy:** Aligning IT services with business goals and customer needs.

   - **Service Design:** Designing new or changed services to meet business requirements.

   - **Service Transition:** Planning and managing changes to IT services.

   - **Service Operation:** Delivering and managing IT services on a day-to-day basis.

- **Continual Service Improvement (CSI):** Improving services and processes continuously to align with changing business needs and technology advancements.

4. **Processes and Functions:** ITIL defines processes (e.g., incident management, change management) and functions (e.g., service desk, technical management) that are crucial for delivering and supporting IT services effectively.

ITIL Processes Implemented at the Service Desk

- **Incident Management:**

  - **Logging:** Ensure all incidents are logged accurately with sufficient detail.

  - **Categorization and Prioritization:** Classify incidents based on impact and urgency to prioritize resolution efforts effectively.

  - **Resolution:** Follow defined procedures to diagnose, escalate (if necessary), and resolve incidents within agreed-upon SLAs.

- **Request Fulfillment:**

  - **Logging:** Record and track service requests from initiation to completion.

  - **Authorization:** Verify user authorization and escalate requests as needed.

  - **Fulfillment:** Use standardized procedures to fulfill requests promptly, ensuring user satisfaction.

- **Problem Management:**

  - **Reporting:** Collaborate with other IT teams to identify and report recurring issues.

  - **Root Cause Analysis:** Assist in gathering data and providing insights for root cause analysis.

  - **Workarounds:** Implement temporary workarounds to minimize impact while permanent solutions are developed.

Adherence to ITIL Service Operation Principles

- **Service Desk Functions:**

  - **Service Level Management:** Ensure service desk operations align with agreed SLAs and OLAs.

  - **IT Operations Management:** Coordinate with IT operations to monitor infrastructure health and performance, escalating issues as necessary.

  - **Technical Management:** Collaborate with technical teams for complex incident and problem resolution.

- **Continuous Improvement (CSI):**

  - **Measurement:** Track and analyze service desk metrics (e.g., average response time, average resolution time) to identify areas for improvement.

  - **Feedback:** Gather user feedback to understand satisfaction levels and identify opportunities for enhancement the quality of the service.

- ○ **Process Review:** Regularly review and update service desk processes based on feedback, trend and performance data.

Benefits of Applying ITIL to Service Desk Operations

- **Enhanced Service Quality:** Standardized processes and procedures lead to consistent service delivery and improved customer satisfaction.

- **Efficiency:** Streamlined workflows and automation reduce resolution times and operational costs.

- **Risk Reduction:** Proactive incident and problem management mitigate risks and prevent service disruptions.

- **Business Alignment:** Service desk operations are aligned with business goals and objectives, supporting organizational success.

Challenges and Considerations

- **Cultural Change:** Implementing ITIL practices may require cultural adjustments within the service desk and broader IT organization.

- **Training and Skills Development:** Service desk staff need ongoing training to understand and apply ITIL principles effectively.

- **Integration with Tools:** Ensure service desk tools and technologies support ITIL processes and facilitate efficient service management.

1. Best Practices for Incident Management

Implementing best practices for incident management is crucial for minimizing disruption to business operations and ensuring timely resolution of IT issues. Here are some key best practices to follow:

1. Incident Identification and Logging

- **Prompt Logging:** Encourage users to report incidents promptly through a centralized service desk or self-service portal.

- **Clear Logging Procedures:** Define clear guidelines for documenting incident details, including symptoms, affected systems, and user impact.

- **Automated Logging:** Utilize monitoring tools to automatically generate incidents based on predefined thresholds or alerts.

2. Classification and Initial Support

- **Categorization:** Classify incidents based on impact and urgency to prioritize resolution efforts effectively.

- **Initial Diagnosis:** Provide frontline support staff with documented procedures and knowledge bases to facilitate initial troubleshooting and diagnosis.

- **Escalation Pathways:** Establish clear escalation paths for incidents that cannot be resolved within agreed-upon service levels.

3. Prioritization and Response

- **Priority Assignment:** Define criteria for assigning incident priorities (e.g., business impact, number of affected users) to ensure appropriate resource allocation.

- **Timely Response:** Adhere to predefined response time targets based on incident priority levels (e.g., high-priority incidents require immediate response).

4. Incident Investigation and Diagnosis

- **Root Cause Analysis:** Conduct thorough root cause analysis (RCA) for major incidents to identify underlying issues and prevent recurrence through problem management process.

- **Documentation:** Gather and maintain detailed incident records, including investigation findings, actions taken, and resolutions applied and all the evidence.

- **Collaboration:** Collaboration among support teams, including technical specialists and subject matter experts, for complex incident resolution.

5. Incident Resolution and Closure

- **Resolution Documentation:** Document resolution steps and communicate them clearly to users and all the stakeholders.

- **User Confirmation:** Obtain user confirmation that the incident has been resolved satisfactorily before closing the incident.

- **Closure Procedures:** Follow formal closure procedures to ensure all necessary documentation and follow-up actions (if any) are completed.

6. Continuous Improvement

- **Post-Incident Review:** Conduct post-incident reviews (PIRs) to analyze the effectiveness of incident response and identify opportunities for improvement.

- **Feedback Loop:** Use insights from PIRs to update incident management processes, training materials, and knowledge bases.

- **Metrics and KPIs:** Monitor incident management metrics (e.g., mean time to resolve, first call resolution rate) to measure performance and drive continuous improvement efforts.

7. Communication and Stakeholder Management

- **Proactive Communication:** Maintain regular communication with users and stakeholders throughout the incident lifecycle, providing updates on progress and resolution status.

- **Manage Expectations:** Set realistic expectations regarding incident resolution times and keep stakeholders informed of any changes or delays.

- **Escalation Management:** Establish escalation procedures for incidents requiring higher-level management involvement or external vendor support.

8. Training and Skills Development

- **Continuous Training:** Provide ongoing training and professional development opportunities for support staff to enhance technical skills and incident management capabilities.

- **Cross-Training:** Encourage cross-training across support teams to ensure flexibility and resilience in handling different types of incidents.

Logging Incidents

Purpose: Prompt and accurate logging of incidents ensures that IT support teams are aware of issues as they arise, allowing for timely resolution.

Best Practices:

- **Centralized Logging:** Establish a centralized system (such as a service desk or incident management tool) where all incidents are logged.

- **User-Friendly Interface:** Ensure the logging interface is intuitive and easily accessible to encourage users to report incidents promptly.

- **Required Information:** Define mandatory fields for incident logging, including:

  - **Affected Service/Device:** Specify the service or device experiencing issues.

  - **Incident Description:** Encourage users to provide a clear and detailed description of the issue, including symptoms and any error messages with steps to reproduce if any.

- ○ **Contact Information:** Capture user contact details for follow-up and communication.

- **Automation:** Integrate monitoring tools to automatically generate incidents based on predefined thresholds or alerts, reducing manual entry errors and ensuring swift detection of issues.

2. Categorizing Incidents

Purpose: Categorization helps in grouping incidents based on their characteristics and allows for efficient handling and prioritization.

Best Practices:

- **Standardized Categories:** Define a set of standardized incident categories and subcategories that align with the organization's IT services and infrastructure.

- **Consistent Use:** Ensure consistent use of categories by providing guidelines and training to support staff.

- **Granularity:** Balance between having enough categories to differentiate incidents effectively without creating an overly complex classification system.

- **Dynamic Updates:** Regularly review and update categories to reflect changes in technology and business requirements.

3. Prioritizing Incidents

Purpose: Prioritization ensures that incidents are addressed based on their impact and urgency, optimizing resource allocation and response times.

Best Practices:

- **Priority Matrix:** Develop a priority matrix that defines criteria for assigning incident priorities, considering:

    - **Impact:** Evaluate the extent to which the incident disrupts business operations or affects users.

    - **Urgency:** Assess the timeframe within which the incident needs to be resolved to minimize further impact.

- **SLA Alignment:** Align incident prioritization with Service Level Agreements (SLAs) to meet agreed-upon response and resolution targets.

- **Escalation Criteria:** Establish clear escalation paths for incidents that require higher-level attention based on their priority levels.

- **Continuous Monitoring:** Monitor incident statuses and adjust priorities as new information becomes available or circumstances change.

Integration and Automation:

- **Integration:** Integrate incident logging, categorization, and prioritization processes with other ITSM (IT Service Management) processes such as Change Management and

Problem Management to ensure seamless coordination and resolution.

- **Automation:** Utilize automation tools to streamline incident handling, such as automated incident categorization based on predefined rules or automated assignment of priorities based on impact and urgency assessments.

Incident Resolution and Closure

Incident resolution and closure are critical phases in the incident management process. Proper handling ensures that incidents are resolved promptly, users are satisfied, and lessons are learned for future improvements. Here are best practices for incident resolution and closure:

Incident Resolution

- **Diagnosis and Investigation:**
  - **Root Cause Analysis (RCA):** Conduct a thorough investigation to identify the underlying cause of the incident.
  - **Technical Support:** Engage technical specialists or subject matter experts as needed to assist in diagnosis and resolution.
  - **Documentation:** Document all steps taken during the investigation and any findings related to the incident.

- **Resolution Steps:**

  - **Follow Standard Procedures:** Adhere to documented incident resolution procedures to ensure consistency and reliability.

  - **Timely Updates:** Provide regular updates to stakeholders and users on the progress of incident resolution.

  - **Communication:** Maintain open communication channels with stakeholders, keeping them informed of any challenges or delays.

- **Workarounds:**

  - **Temporary Fixes:** Implement temporary workarounds if immediate resolution is not feasible to minimize impact on business operations.

  - **Monitoring:** Monitor the effectiveness of workarounds and escalate if they prove insufficient or lead to additional issues.

Incident Closure

1. **Verification:**

   - **User Confirmation:** Obtain confirmation from users that the incident has been resolved to their satisfaction.

   - **Functional Testing:** Conduct functional testing, if applicable, to ensure that the affected service or system is functioning correctly.

2. **Documentation and Closure:**

   - **Documentation:** Document the final resolution steps, including any workarounds applied and lessons learned during the incident resolution process.

   - **Closure Procedures:** Follow formal closure procedures in the incident management system to mark the incident as resolved.

3. **Review and Analysis:**

   - **Post-Incident Review (PIR):** Conduct a post-incident review to analyze the incident management process, identify root causes, and determine if any improvements are needed.

   - **Lessons Learned:** Capture lessons learned from the incident to improve future incident response and prevent similar incidents from occurring.

Best Practices for Incident Resolution and Closure

- **Adhere to SLAs:** Ensure that incident resolution and closure timelines align with agreed Service Level Agreements (SLAs).

- **Continuous Improvement:** Use insights from incident resolution and closure to refine incident management processes and procedures continuously.

- **User Satisfaction:** Prioritize user satisfaction by providing clear communication, timely updates, and effective resolution.

- **Knowledge Management:** Update knowledge bases and documentation with resolved incidents and their resolutions for future reference.

Chapter Summary – Mindmap

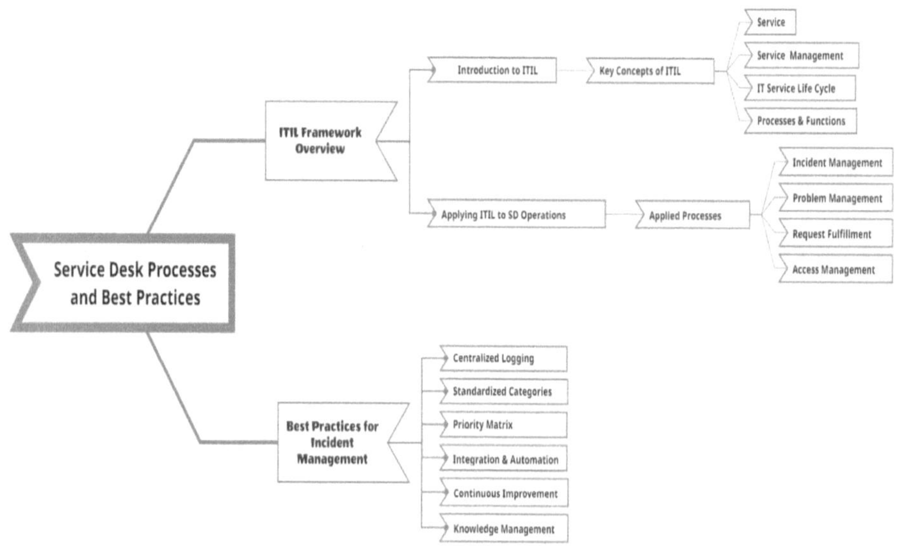

Chapter 5

Delivering Exceptional Customer Service

Delivering outstanding customer support service is vital aspect in building long-term customer relationships, enhancing brand loyalty, and establishing positive word-of-mouth. Here are key strategies and best practices to ensure exceptional customer service:

1. **Understand Customer Needs:** Active listening, asking questions, and regularly seeking customer feedback are essential for understanding customer needs.

2. **Communication Skills:** Clarity, conciseness, empathy, and positive language are the key components of effective communication.

3. **Consistency and Reliability:** Maintain consistency across all channels, be reliable by keeping promises, and respond promptly.

4. **Empowerment and Ownership:** Empower your team to make decisions and encourage them to take ownership of issues until they are resolved.

5. **Knowledge and Training:** Continuously provide training on product updates, new technologies, and processes.

6. **Personalization:** Personalize customer interactions by considering their local culture, using their names, and referencing past interactions when appropriate.

7. **Handling Complaints and Issues:** Stay calm and composed, listen first, acknowledge, and apologize for any inconvenience. Focus on resolving the issue and follow up to ensure customer satisfaction.

8. **Technology and Tools:** Establish multichannel interactions and provide self-service options with FAQs and discussion forums.

9. **Customer-Centric Culture:** Foster a customer-centric culture and reward employees who exemplify it.

10. **Continuous Improvement:** Utilize customer feedback and encourage innovation to drive continuous improvement.

Practical Steps for Implementation

1. **Customer Service Training:** Conduct regular training sessions focused on communication skills, empathy, and problem-solving.

2. **Customer Service Standards:** Design and implement clear customer service standards and guidelines as part of SOP's.

3. **Performance Metrics:** Track key performance metrics such as response time, resolution time, and customer satisfaction scores.

4. **Customer Feedback Systems:** Establish systems to collect and analyze customer feedback regularly.

5. **Empowerment Programs:** Create programs that empower employees to make decisions and recognize their efforts in delivering exceptional service.

5.1 Customer Service Fundamentals

Customer service fundamentals for an IT service desk team include active listening, clear communication, and empathy. It's essential to understand and address customer needs promptly while maintaining a positive attitude.

Effective problem-solving skills and a thorough knowledge of IT systems are crucial. Regular training on new technologies and processes helps in staying updated.

Encouraging team members to take ownership of issues until resolved and fostering a customer-centric culture with recognition for excellent service are key practices. Utilizing customer feedback and promoting innovation ensures continuous improvement and high-quality service delivery.

5.1.1 Understanding Customer Needs

Understanding customer needs is crucial for delivering exceptional customer service, creating products that meet market demands, and fostering long-term customer loyalty. Here are strategies and best practices to effectively understand and address customer needs:

1. Active Listening

- **Focus on the Customer:** Give your full attention to the customer during interactions. Avoid distractions and listen carefully to what they are saying.

- **Ask Clarifying Questions:** To ensure you understand the customer's needs and concerns, ask questions that clarify their points.

- **Summarize and Reflect:** Repeat back what you've heard to confirm understanding. This shows the customer that you are listening and values their input.

2. Gather Customer Feedback

- **Surveys and Questionnaires:** Use surveys to collect structured feedback from customers about their experiences and needs.

- **Customer Interviews:** Conduct one-on-one interviews to gain deeper insights into customer perspectives and preferences.

- **Focus Groups:** Organize focus groups to discuss products, services, and customer expectations in detail.

3. Analyze Customer Data

- **CRM Systems:** Utilize Customer Relationship Management (CRM) systems to track customer interactions, preferences, and purchase history.

- **Data Analytics:** Analyze customer data to identify patterns, trends, and insights that can inform decision-making.

- **Segmentation:** Segment your customer base into different groups based on statistics, behavior, and preferences to tailor your approach.

4. Discussion forums

- **Social Listening:** Monitor discussion forum platforms for mentions of your brand, products, and services. Pay attention to customer comments and discussions.

5. Empathy Mapping

- **Empathy Maps:** Create empathy maps to visualize what customers are thinking, feeling, saying, and doing. This helps in understanding their emotional and rational needs.

- **Customer Journeys:** Map out customer journeys to identify touchpoints and potential pain points throughout their interaction with your brand.

6. Personalize Interactions

- **Tailored Communication:** Use customer data to personalize interactions. Address customers by name and reference previous interactions or purchases.

- **Customized Solutions:** Offer solutions and recommendations that are specifically tailored to the customer's unique needs and preferences.

7. Observe Customer Behavior

- **In-Store Observations:** If applicable, observe how customers interact with products in-store to gain insights into their preferences and behaviors.

- **Website Analytics:** Use web analytics tools to track customer behavior on your website, such as navigation patterns, popular pages, and time spent on specific content.

8. Competitive Analysis

- **Benchmarking:** Compare your products, services, and customer experiences with those of competitors to identify gaps and opportunities.

- **Customer Insights:** Analyze competitor reviews and feedback to understand what customers like or dislike about similar offerings.

9. Engage with Customer Communities

- **Online Communities:** Participate in online forums, communities, and social media groups where your customers are active.

- **Customer Advisory Boards:** Establish customer advisory boards to gather direct input from key customers on product development and service improvements.

10. Continual Learning and Adaptation

- **Continuous Improvement:** Regularly review and update your understanding of customer needs as they evolve. Stay informed about industry trends and changes in customer behavior.

- **Agile Approach:** Adopt an agile approach to quickly adapt to changing customer needs and preferences.

Practical Steps for Implementation

- **Feedback Channels:** Establish multiple channels for customers to provide feedback, such as surveys, suggestion boxes, and social media.

- **Regular Training:** Train staff on active listening, empathy, and effective communication skills.

- **CRM Utilization:** Implement or optimize CRM systems to capture and analyze customer data effectively.

- **Customer Engagement:** Regularly engage with customers through various channels to maintain an ongoing understanding of their needs.

- **Iterative Processes:** Continuously iterate on products and services based on customer feedback and data insights.

5.1.2 Effective Communication Skills

Effective communication skills are essential for delivering exceptional customer service, fostering teamwork, and ensuring clear and efficient interactions. Here are the key components of effective communication and strategies to improve them:

1. Active Listening

- **Full Attention:** Give your full attention to the speaker without interrupting. Avoid distractions and focus on what the person is saying.

- **Show Engagement:** Use non-verbal cues like nodding, maintaining eye contact, and leaning slightly forward to show that you are engaged.

- **Clarification:** Ask clarifying questions to ensure you understand the message correctly. For example, "Could you please elaborate on that point?"

- **Paraphrasing:** Repeat back what you've heard in your own words to confirm understanding. For example, "So, what you're saying is..."

2. Clear and Concise Communication

- **Simple Language:** Use clear and straightforward language. Avoid jargon or technical terms that might confuse the listener.

- **Brevity:** Keep your messages concise and to the point. Avoid overloading the listener with unnecessary information.

- **Structured Information:** Present information in a logical sequence, making it easier for the listener to follow.

3. Empathy and Understanding

- **Empathetic Statements:** Show empathy by acknowledging the listener's feelings and perspectives. For example, "I understand how that situation could be frustrating."

- **Respect:** Treat the listener with respect and consideration, regardless of the context of the communication.

4. Non-Verbal Communication

- **Body Language:** Be aware of your body language. Open, relaxed postures convey openness and attentiveness.

- **Facial Expressions:** Use appropriate facial expressions to match your message and show understanding and engagement.

- **Tone of Voice:** Ensure your tone of voice matches the message. A warm and friendly tone can help build rapport and trust.

5. Asking Effective Questions

- **Open-Ended Questions:** Use open-ended questions to encourage detailed responses. For example, "Can you tell me more about...?"

- **Closed-Ended Questions:** Use closed-ended questions when you need specific information. For example, "Did you receive the email I sent yesterday?"

6. Providing Clear Feedback

- **Constructive Feedback:** Offer feedback that is specific, actionable, and focused on improvement. For example, "I noticed that you did X, which was great. Next time, try to focus more on Y."

- **Positive Reinforcement:** Recognize and praise positive behaviors and achievements. This motivates and encourages the listener.

7. Adaptability

- **Tailoring Communication:** Adapt your communication style to suit the listener's preferences and the context. For example, some people may prefer detailed explanations, while others may prefer a brief overview.

- **Cultural Sensitivity:** Be aware of cultural differences and adjust your communication style accordingly to avoid misunderstandings.

8. Managing Conflicts

- **Stay Calm:** Keep a calm and composed demeanor during conflicts or disagreements.

- **Listen Actively:** Listen to the other person's perspective without interrupting.

- **Seek Solutions:** Focus on finding mutually acceptable solutions rather than assigning blame.

9. Building Rapport

- **Common Ground:** Find common ground and shared interests to build rapport with the listener.

- **Personal Touch:** Use the listener's name and reference previous conversations or interactions to personalize the communication.

10. Continuous Improvement

- **Self-Reflection:** Regularly reflect on your communication experiences and identify areas for improvement.

- **Feedback:** Seek feedback from others on your communication skills and be open to adjusting.

- **Training:** Participate in communication skills training and workshops to continuously improve your abilities.

Practical Steps for Implementation

1. **Active Listening Practice:** Regularly practice active listening in both personal and professional settings to enhance your skills.

2. **Clear Communication Exercises:** Engage in exercises that focus on delivering clear and concise messages, such as summarizing complex information in a few sentences.

3. **Empathy Development:** Participate in role-playing exercises to develop and demonstrate empathy in various scenarios.

4. **Non-Verbal Awareness:** Record and review your conversations to become more aware of your non-verbal communication cues.

5. **Adaptability Drills:** Practice adapting your communication style with different types of people and in various contexts.

6. **Conflict Resolution Workshops:** Attend workshops or training sessions on conflict resolution to learn effective strategies for managing disagreements.

7. **Feedback Mechanisms:** Set up regular feedback mechanisms with colleagues and customers to gather input on your communication effectiveness.

5.2 Handling Difficult Situations

Handling difficult situations effectively is a vital skill for maintaining positive relationships, ensuring customer satisfaction, and fostering a collaborative work environment. Here are key strategies and best practices for managing challenging interactions:

1. Stay Calm and Composed

- **Maintain Composure:** Keep your emotions in check and stay calm, even if the other person is upset or angry.

- **Deep Breathing:** Use deep breathing techniques to help maintain your composure and reduce stress.

- **Pause Before Responding:** Take a moment to gather your thoughts before responding to ensure a measured and thoughtful reply.

2. Active Listening

- **Full Attention:** Listen attentively to the other person without interrupting. Show that you are fully engaged and understand their perspective.

- **Acknowledge Feelings:** Validate the other person's emotions by acknowledging their feelings. For example, "I can see that you're frustrated, and I understand why."

- **Paraphrase:** Repeat back what you've heard in your own words to confirm understanding and demonstrate empathy. For example, "So, you're saying that you're unhappy with the service you received?"

3. Empathy and Understanding

- **Show Empathy:** Express genuine concern and empathy for the other person's situation. For example, "I'm sorry to hear that you're experiencing this issue."

- **Put Yourself in Their Shoes:** Try to understand the situation from the other person's perspective to gain a deeper understanding of their concerns.

4. Effective Communication

- **Clear and Concise:** Communicate your points clearly and concisely, avoiding jargon or complex language.

- **Positive Language:** Use positive and constructive language to create a more favorable outcome. For example, instead of saying "I can't do that," say "Here's what I can do for you."

- **Stay Professional:** Maintain a professional tone and demeanor throughout the interaction, regardless of the other person's behavior.

5. Problem-Solving

- **Identify the Root Cause:** Work to identify the underlying cause of the issue, rather than just addressing the symptoms.

- **Collaborative Solutions:** Involve the other person in finding a solution. Ask for their input and work together to come up with a resolution. For example, "What do you think would be a fair solution to this problem?"

- **Offer Solutions:** Provide practical and viable solutions to address the issue. Clearly explain the steps involved in resolving the problem.

6. Taking Responsibility

- **Own the Issue:** Take responsibility for the problem, even if it wasn't directly caused by you. For example, "I apologize for the inconvenience this has caused. Let's work together to resolve it."

- **Sincere Apology:** Offer a sincere and genuine apology if the situation warrants it. For example, "I'm truly sorry for the inconvenience and frustration this has caused you."

7. Setting Boundaries

- **Respectfully Set Limits:** If the conversation becomes hostile or abusive, respectfully set boundaries. For example, "I want to help you, but I need you to speak to me respectfully so we can resolve this together."

- **Know When to Escalate:** Recognize when the situation requires escalation to a higher authority or another team member.

8. Follow-Up

- **Ensure Resolution:** Follow up with the person to ensure that the issue has been fully resolved and that they are satisfied with the outcome.

- **Continuous Communication:** Keep the lines of communication open and provide updates if the resolution takes time.

Practical Steps for Implementation

1. **Training Sessions:** Conduct regular training sessions on conflict resolution and handling difficult situations.

2. **Role-Playing:** Practice handling difficult situations through role-playing exercises to build confidence and skills.

3. **Stress Management:** Teach stress management techniques to help employees stay calm under pressure.

4. **Feedback Mechanisms:** Set up mechanisms to gather feedback on how difficult situations are handled and identify areas for improvement.

5. **Support Systems:** Provide support systems, such as access to supervisors or mentors, for employees dealing with particularly challenging situations.

6. **Documentation:** Keep detailed records of difficult interactions to identify patterns and develop strategies for handling similar situations in the future.

5.2.1 Dealing with Challenging Customers

Dealing with challenging customers requires patience, empathy, and effective communication skills. Here are strategies and best practices to handle difficult customer interactions successfully:

1. Stay Calm and Professional

- **Maintain Composure:** Keep your emotions in check and remain calm, regardless of the customer's behavior. Deep breathing and a moment of pause can help you stay composed.

- **Professional Demeanor:** Maintain a professional tone and body language, even if the customer is upset or confrontational.

2. Active Listening

- **Full Attention:** Give the customer your full attention and avoid interrupting them. Let them express their concerns fully before responding.

- **Acknowledge Feelings:** Show empathy by acknowledging the customer's emotions. For example, "I understand that you're frustrated, and I'm here to help."

- **Paraphrase:** Repeat back what you've heard to confirm understanding and demonstrate that you are listening. For example, "So, you're saying that your order arrived late and damaged?"

3. Show Empathy and Understanding

- **Empathetic Statements:** Use empathetic language to show that you care about the customer's experience. For example, "I'm really sorry to hear that you had a negative experience."

- **Put Yourself in Their Shoes:** Try to see the situation from the customer's perspective to better understand their concerns and frustrations.

4. Effective Communication

- **Clear and Concise:** Communicate your points clearly and concisely. Avoid using jargon or overly technical language.

- **Positive Language:** Use positive and solution-focused language. Instead of saying "I can't do that," say "Here's what I can do to help."

- **Stay Professional:** Maintain a respectful and courteous tone throughout the interaction.

5. Problem-Solving

- **Identify the Root Cause:** Work to identify the underlying cause of the customer's issue. Ask questions to gather more information if needed.

- **Collaborative Solutions:** Involve the customer in finding a solution. Ask for their input and work together to resolve the issue. For example, "What would be an acceptable resolution for you?"

- **Offer Solutions:** Provide practical and actionable solutions to address the customer's concerns. Clearly explain the steps involved in resolving the problem.

6. Taking Responsibility

- **Own the Issue:** Take responsibility for resolving the customer's issue, even if it wasn't directly caused by you. For example, "I apologize for the inconvenience this has caused. Let's work together to resolve it."

- **Sincere Apology:** Offer a genuine apology if the situation warrants it. For example, "I'm truly sorry for the inconvenience and frustration this has caused you."

7. Setting Boundaries

- **Respectfully Set Limits:** If the customer becomes abusive or hostile, set boundaries respectfully. For example, "I want to help you, but I need you to speak to me respectfully so we can resolve this together."

- **Know When to Escalate:** Recognize when the situation requires escalation to a higher authority or another team member.

8. Follow-Up

- **Ensure Resolution:** Follow up with the customer to ensure that the issue has been fully resolved and that they are satisfied with the outcome.

- **Continuous Communication:** Keep the lines of communication open and provide updates if the resolution takes time.

Practical Steps for Implementation

1. **Training Sessions:** Conduct regular training sessions on handling challenging customers and conflict resolution.

2. **Role-Playing:** Practice dealing with difficult customer scenarios through role-playing exercises to build confidence and skills.

3. **Stress Management:** Teach stress management techniques to help employees stay calm under pressure.

4. **Feedback Mechanisms:** Set up mechanisms to gather feedback on how difficult customer interactions are handled and identify areas for improvement.

5. **Support Systems:** Provide support systems, such as access to supervisors or mentors, for employees dealing with particularly challenging customers.

6. **Documentation:** Keep detailed records of difficult interactions to identify patterns and develop strategies for handling similar situations in the future.

5.2.2 Conflict Resolution Strategies

Conflict resolution strategies are essential for maintaining a positive and productive environment, whether in customer service, within teams, or in personal relationships. Here are effective strategies to resolve conflicts:

1. Stay Calm and Composed

- **Maintain Composure:** Keep your emotions in check and remain calm, regardless of the situation. Deep breathing or taking a short pause can help you stay composed.

- **Professional Demeanor:** Maintain a professional tone and body language, even if others are upset or confrontational.

2. Active Listening

- **Full Attention:** Give the other party your full attention and avoid interrupting them. Let them express their concerns fully before responding.

- **Acknowledge Feelings:** Show empathy by acknowledging the other party's emotions. For example, "I understand that you're upset, and I'm here to help."

- **Paraphrase:** Repeat back what you've heard to confirm understanding and demonstrate that you are listening. For example, "So, you're saying that you feel your workload is unfairly distributed?"

3. Empathy and Understanding

- **Show Empathy:** Express genuine concern and empathy for the other person's situation. For example, "I'm really sorry that you're feeling this way."

- **Perspective-Taking:** Try to see the situation from the other person's perspective to better understand their concerns and frustrations.

4. Clear and Concise Communication

- **Simple Language:** Use clear and straightforward language to avoid misunderstandings.

- **Positive Language:** Use positive and constructive language to create a more favorable outcome. Instead of saying "I can't do that," say "Here's what I can do for you."

- **Stay Professional:** Maintain a respectful and courteous tone throughout the interaction.

5. Problem-Solving

- **Identify the Root Cause:** Work to identify the underlying cause of the conflict. Ask questions to gather more information if needed.

- **Collaborative Solutions:** Involve the other party in finding a solution. Ask for their input and work together to resolve the issue. For example, "What do you think would be a fair solution to this problem?"

- **Offer Solutions:** Provide practical and actionable solutions to address the conflict. Clearly explain the steps involved in resolving the problem.

6. Taking Responsibility

- **Own the Issue:** Take responsibility for resolving the conflict, even if it wasn't directly caused by you. For example, "I apologize for any misunderstanding. Let's work together to resolve it."

- **Sincere Apology:** Offer a genuine apology if the situation warrants it. For example, "I'm truly sorry for the inconvenience and frustration this has caused you."

7. Setting Boundaries

- **Respectfully Set Limits:** If the conversation becomes hostile or abusive, respectfully set boundaries. For example, "I want to help you, but I need you to speak to me respectfully so we can resolve this together."

- **Know When to Escalate:** Recognize when the situation requires escalation to a higher authority or another team member.

8. Follow-Up

- **Ensure Resolution:** Follow up with the other party to ensure that the issue has been fully resolved and that they are satisfied with the outcome.

- **Continuous Communication:** Keep the lines of communication open and provide updates if the resolution takes time.

9. Mediation

- **Neutral Third Party:** Involve a neutral third party to mediate the conflict if necessary. This can help facilitate a fair and unbiased resolution.

- **Structured Mediation Process:** Use a structured mediation process to ensure all parties have an opportunity to express their views and work towards a mutually acceptable solution.

10. Continuous Improvement

- **Feedback Mechanisms:** Set up mechanisms to gather feedback on how conflicts are handled and identify areas for improvement.

- **Training:** Provide training on conflict resolution and effective communication skills.

- **Support Systems:** Provide access to resources, such as counselors or mediators, for ongoing support in managing conflicts.

Practical Steps for Implementation

1. **Conflict Resolution Training:** Conduct regular training sessions on conflict resolution and effective communication.

2. **Role-Playing:** Practice handling conflict scenarios through role-playing exercises to build confidence and skills.

3. **Stress Management:** Teach stress management techniques to help individuals stay calm under pressure.

4. **Feedback Mechanisms:** Set up mechanisms to gather feedback on how conflicts are handled and identify areas for improvement.

5. **Support Systems:** Provide access to support systems, such as counselors or mediators, for individuals dealing with conflicts.

6. **Documentation:** Keep detailed records of conflicts and resolutions to identify patterns and develop strategies for handling similar situations in the future.

Chapter Summary – Mindmap

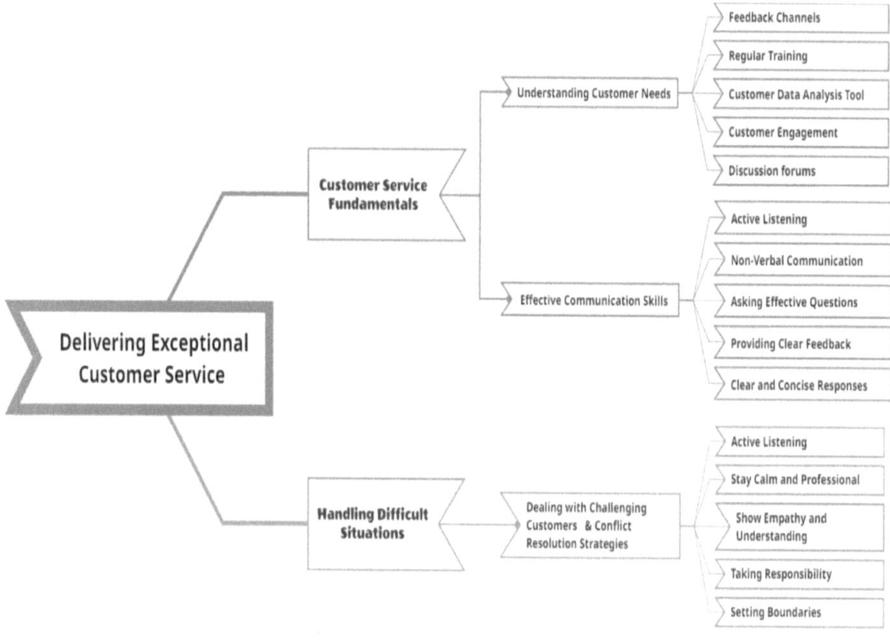

Chapter 6

Continuous Improvement and Learning

Continuous improvement and learning are essential for personal and organizational growth. By establishing a culture of continuous improvement, organizations can enhance their processes, products, and services, while individuals can develop their knowledge and skills. Here are key strategies and best practices for continuous improvement and learning:

1. Embrace a Growth Mindset

- **Cultivate a Growth Mindset:** Encourage a mindset that values learning and sees challenges as opportunities for growth. Emphasize that abilities and intelligence can be developed through consistent learning and applying the learnings.

- **Encourage Curiosity:** Promote and encourage environment where asking questions are appreciated.

2. Set Clear Goals and Objectives

- **Define Objectives:** Set clear, measurable goals for both personal and organizational improvement and growth.

Use SMART criteria (Specific, Measurable, Achievable, Relevant, Time-bound) to ensure goals are well-defined.

- **Regular Review:** Periodically review and adjust goals to ensure they remain relevant and aligned with overall objectives and roadmaps.

3. Develop a Learning Culture

- **Provide Training and Development:** Plan regular training and development opportunities to staffs. This can include workshops, seminars, online courses, and certifications.

- **Encourage Knowledge Sharing:** Create platforms for employees to share knowledge and best practices, such as internal wikis, knowledge bases, and regular team meetings.

- **Support Learning Initiatives:** Encourage and support initiatives like book clubs, Team lunch-and-learning sessions, and cross-departmental projects to promote learning and collaboration.

4. Implement Continuous Improvement Processes

- **Adopt Improvement Methodologies:** Use proven methodologies such as Lean, Six Sigma, or Kaizen to systematically identify and eliminate inefficiencies.

- **Regular Audits and Reviews:** Conduct regular audits and reviews of processes, products, and services to identify areas for improvement.

- **Employee Involvement:** Involve employees at all levels in the improvement process. Encourage them to identify problems and brainstorm and come up with best possible solutions.

5. Use Data and Feedback

- **Collect Data:** Gather data on performance metrics and use it to identify trends, patterns, and areas needing improvement.

- **Solicit Feedback:** Regularly collect feedback from employees, customers, and stakeholders. Use surveys, suggestion boxes, and focus groups to gather insights.

- **Analyze and Act:** Analyze the collected data and feedback to make informed decisions. Implement changes based on the insights gained.

6. Encourage Innovation and Experimentation

- **Support Innovation:** Encourage employees to think creatively and come up with new ideas. Provide resources and support for experimentation and innovation.

- **Pilot Projects:** Implement pilot projects to test new ideas and approaches on a small scale before rolling them out more broadly.

- **Learn from Failures:** Treat failures as learning opportunities. Analyze what went wrong, adjust, and try again.

7. Recognize and Reward Improvement

- **Celebrate Successes:** Recognize and celebrate improvements and successes, both big and small. This can be done through awards, public recognition, or other incentives.

- **Reward Efforts:** Provide rewards for employees who contribute to continuous improvement efforts. This can include bonuses, gift vouchers, or other forms of recognition including promotion.

8. Develop Leadership and Mentoring

- **Leadership Training:** Provide training for leaders to develop their skills in managing change, encouraging innovation, and supporting continuous improvement.

- **Mentoring Programs:** Implement mentoring programs to pair experienced employees with those who are looking to develop their skills and knowledge.

9. Use Technology and Tools

- **Leverage Technology:** Use technology to streamline processes, enhance productivity, and facilitate learning. This can include project management tools, e-learning platforms, and collaboration software.

- **Automation:** Automate repetitive tasks to free up time for more valuable activities and continuous improvement efforts.

10. Create a Continuous Improvement Plan

- **Document the Plan:** Create a formal continuous improvement plan that outlines goals, strategies, and actions to be taken.

- **Monitor Progress:** Regularly monitor progress against the plan and adjust as needed.

- **Engage Stakeholders:** Make sure that all relevant stakeholders are engaged in the continuous improvement process and understand their roles and responsibilities.

Practical Steps for Implementation

1. **Training Programs:** Develop and implement ongoing training programs for employees at all levels.

2. **Feedback Mechanisms:** Establish mechanisms for gathering and analyzing feedback from employees, customers, and stakeholders.

3. **Regular Reviews:** Schedule regular reviews of processes, products, and services to identify areas for improvement.

4. **Innovation Labs:** Create dedicated spaces or times for employees to brainstorm and test new ideas.

5. **Recognition Programs:** Implement programs to recognize and reward employees who contribute to continuous improvement efforts.

6. **Mentoring and Coaching:** Set up mentoring and coaching programs to support employee development.

- **Technology Upgrades:** Invest in technology and tools that support continuous improvement and learning initiatives.

6.1 Feedback and Quality Assurance

Feedback and quality assurance are crucial components in maintaining and improving the standards of services, products, and processes within an organization. By effectively gathering, analyzing, and acting on feedback, and by implementing robust quality assurance practices, organizations can ensure they meet and exceed expectations. Here are strategies and best practices for managing feedback and quality assurance:

1. Establish a Feedback Loop

- **Collect Feedback:** Implement multiple channels for collecting feedback from customers, employees, and stakeholders, such as surveys, suggestion boxes, online reviews, and direct interviews.

- **Analyze Feedback:** Regularly review and analyze the feedback to identify common themes, issues, and areas for improvement.

- **Act on Feedback:** Develop action plans based on feedback to address identified issues and improve products, services, and processes.

- **Communicate Changes:** Inform relevant parties about the changes made in response to their feedback, demonstrating that their input is valued and has an impact.

2. Implement Quality Assurance Processes

- **Define Quality Standards:** Standards for quality and expectations should be clearly defined for products, processes, and services, ensuring alignment with customer expectations and industry best practices.

- **Develop QA Procedures:** Establish quality assurance procedures, including regular inspections, audits, and testing, to ensure standards are consistently met.

- **Use Checklists and Templates:** Develop checklists and templates to standardize quality assurance processes and ensure consistency across the organization.

- **Document Findings:** Maintain detailed records of QA inspections, audits, and tests to track performance and identify trends over time.

3. Continuous Improvement

- **Identifying Pain Points:** Collaborate with Service Desk Analysts (SDAs) to understand their pain points and challenges with the current processes, tools, and templates, and identify areas for improvement.

- **Identify Improvement Areas:** Use feedback and QA data to identify areas for continuous improvement. Focus on processes, products, and services that have the greatest impact operational efficiency and customer satisfaction.

- **Implement Improvements:** Develop and implement improvement plans, using methodologies such as PDCA (Plan-Do-Check-Act).

- **Monitor Results:** Continuously monitor the results of improvement initiatives to ensure they are effective and make further adjustments on need basis.

4. Employee Involvement

- **Encourage Participation:** Involve employees at all levels in the feedback and quality assurance processes. Encourage them to share their insights and suggestions for improvement.

- **Training and Development:** Provide training on quality assurance practices and the importance of feedback. Ensure employees have the skills and knowledge needed to contribute effectively.

- **Recognition and Rewards:** Recognize and reward employees who contribute to quality assurance and continuous improvement efforts.

5. Use Technology and Tools

- **Feedback Management Systems:** Implement feedback management systems to collect, analyze, and act on feedback efficiently. These systems can automate surveys, track responses, and generate reports.

- **Quality Management Software:** Use quality management software to streamline QA processes, track performance, and manage documentation.

- **Data Analytics:** Utilize data analytics tools to gain deeper insights from feedback and QA data, identifying trends and areas for improvement.

6. Benchmarking and Best Practices

- **Benchmarking:** Compare your organization's performance with industry standards and best practices. Identify gaps and areas where your organization can improve.

- **Adopt Best Practices:** Research and adopt best practices from industry leaders and similar organizations to enhance your feedback and quality assurance processes.

7. Regular Review and Updates

- **Periodic Reviews:** Conduct regular reviews of feedback and quality assurance processes to ensure they remain effective and relevant.

- **Update Processes:** Update processes and procedures as needed based on review findings, changes in industry standards, or evolving customer expectations.

Practical Steps for Implementation

1. **Develop Feedback Channels:** Set up multiple channels for collecting feedback, such as online surveys, feedback forms, customer interviews, and suggestion boxes.

2. **Create QA Procedures:** Establish detailed quality assurance procedures, including regular audits, inspections, and testing protocols.

3. **Train Employees:** Provide training on the importance of feedback and quality assurance, and equip employees with the necessary skills and tools.

4. **Implement Technology:** Invest in feedback management systems and quality management software to streamline processes and improve efficiency.

5. **Benchmark Performance:** Regularly benchmark your organization's performance against industry standards and best practices.

6. **Continuous Review:** Schedule regular reviews of feedback and quality assurance processes to ensure they remain effective and aligned with organizational goals.

7. **Communicate Changes:** Keep stakeholders informed about improvements made based on feedback and QA findings, reinforcing the value of their input.

6.1.1 Gathering and Using Customer Feedback

Gathering and effectively using customer feedback is essential for improving products, services, and overall customer satisfaction. Here's a comprehensive guide on how to gather and utilize customer feedback:

Gathering Customer Feedback

1. **Identify Feedback Sources:**

    ○ **Surveys:** Design and distribute surveys through various channels such as email, website pop-ups, or mobile apps. Use both quantitative (rating scales) and qualitative (open-ended questions) formats.

    ○ **Feedback Forms:** Embed feedback forms on your website or within your product/service interface for customers to easily submit their opinions.

- ○ **Social Media:** Monitor mentions, comments, and direct messages on platforms like Twitter, Facebook, and LinkedIn to gather real-time feedback.

- ○ **Customer Interviews:** Conduct one-on-one interviews with select customers to delve deeper into their experiences and opinions.

- ○ **Focus Groups:** Organize focus groups comprising representative customers to gather detailed insights in a structured setting.

2. **Utilize Net Promoter Score (NPS):**

- ○ Implement NPS surveys to measure customer loyalty and gauge the likelihood of customers recommending your business to others.

3. **Monitor Online Reviews:**

- ○ Track reviews on platforms such as Google Reviews, Yelp, and industry-specific review sites to understand customer sentiment and identify areas for improvement.

4. **Customer Support Interactions:**

- ○ Analyze interactions with customer support teams, including complaints and suggestions, as they often highlight recurring issues or customer pain points.

Utilizing Customer Feedback

1. **Organize and Analyze:**

   - Aggregate feedback from various sources into a centralized database or feedback management system.

   - Categorize feedback based on themes or topics to identify common issues or trends.

2. **Prioritize Feedback:**

   - Prioritize feedback based on impact and feasibility. Focus on addressing issues that have the greatest potential to improve customer satisfaction or business performance.

3. **Act Promptly:**

   - Respond to feedback promptly, especially for urgent or critical issues. Acknowledge receipt of feedback and provide timelines for resolution where possible.

4. **Implement Changes:**

   - Develop action plans based on customer feedback. Implement changes to products, services, or processes that address identified issues or enhance the customer experience.

   - Communicate changes to customers to demonstrate that their feedback is valued and to manage expectations.

5. **Monitor Progress:**

   o   Continuously monitor the impact of changes made based on customer feedback. Measure metrics such as customer satisfaction scores, retention rates, and repeat purchase behavior to assess improvements.

6. **Close the Feedback Loop:**

   o   Follow up with customers who provided feedback to inform them of changes made as a result of their input. This reinforces their importance to your business and encourages ongoing engagement.

7. **Iterate and Improve:**

   o   Use customer feedback as a continuous improvement tool. Regularly revisit feedback mechanisms, update surveys, and adjust processes to capture evolving customer needs and expectations.

Best Practices

- **Transparent Communication:** Be transparent with customers about how their feedback is used and the outcomes of their input.

- **Engage Employees:** Involve employees across departments in understanding and acting on customer feedback to establish a customer-centric culture.

- **Regular Review:** Conduct regular reviews of feedback processes and metrics to ensure they remain relevant and effective.

- **Continuous Learning:** Treat customer feedback as a learning opportunity, leveraging insights to innovate and stay ahead of competitors.

6.1.2 Internal Quality Reviews and Audits

Internal quality reviews and audits are critical processes for organizations to assess and improve their operations, products, and services. These reviews help ensure that internal processes meet established standards, identify areas for improvement, and maintain consistency across the organization. Here's a detailed guide on internal quality reviews and audits:

Internal Quality Reviews

1. **Purpose and Objectives:**

   - **Assessment:** Evaluate internal processes, procedures, and outputs to ensure they align with organizational goals and quality standards.

   - **Identification of Gaps:** Identify gaps or discrepancies between current practices and desired outcomes.

   - **Continuous Improvement:** Provide insights for continuous improvement initiatives within the organization.

2. **Types of Internal Quality Reviews:**

   - **Process Reviews:** Assess the effectiveness and efficiency of operational processes, such as production workflows, service delivery processes, or project management methodologies.

- **Product or Service Reviews:** Evaluate the quality and performance of products or services against predefined criteria and customer expectations.

- **Compliance Reviews:** Ensure adherence to regulatory requirements, industry standards, and internal policies.

- **Performance Reviews:** Measure key performance indicators (KPIs) to assess overall organizational performance and identify areas for enhancement.

3. **Steps in Conducting Internal Quality Reviews:**

- **Planning:** Define the scope, objectives, and criteria for the review. Establish a timeline and allocate resources accordingly.

- **Data Collection:** Gather relevant data, documentation, and evidence related to the processes, products, or services under review.

- **Analysis:** Analyze the collected data to identify trends, patterns, strengths, weaknesses, and areas for improvement.

- **Reporting:** Prepare comprehensive reports summarizing findings, observations, and recommendations. Include actionable insights and suggestions for enhancements.

- **Feedback and Action:** Present findings to stakeholders and decision-makers. Develop action plans to address identified issues and implement improvements.

- ○ **Follow-up:** Monitor and track the implementation of corrective actions and improvements. Conduct periodic follow-up reviews to measure progress and effectiveness.

Internal Audits

1. **Purpose and Objectives:**

   - ○ **Verification:** Verify compliance with internal policies, procedures, and regulatory requirements.

   - ○ **Risk Assessment:** Identify potential risks and vulnerabilities within organizational processes and operations.

   - ○ **Improvement Opportunities:** Highlight opportunities for enhancing efficiency, effectiveness, and quality management.

2. **Types of Internal Audits:**

   - ○ **Financial Audits:** Review financial records, transactions, and controls to ensure accuracy and compliance with accounting standards.

   - ○ **Operational Audits:** Evaluate operational processes, systems, and controls to optimize resource utilization and mitigate operational risks.

   - ○ **Compliance Audits:** Assess adherence to legal, regulatory, and contractual obligations.

   - ○ **Information Technology (IT) Audits:** Evaluate IT infrastructure, systems, and security measures to safeguard data integrity and confidentiality.

3. **Steps in Conducting Internal Audits:**

   o **Planning:** Define audit objectives, scope, and criteria. Develop an audit plan outlining activities, timelines, and resource requirements.

   o **Fieldwork:** Collect and examine evidence, conduct interviews, and perform tests to validate compliance and effectiveness.

   o **Reporting:** Prepare audit reports documenting findings, observations, and recommendations. Include management responses and action plans.

   o **Follow-up:** Monitor the implementation of corrective actions and improvements. Validate the effectiveness of measures taken.

   o **Continuous Improvement:** Incorporate lessons learned and audit outcomes into organizational policies, procedures, and practices.

Best Practices for Internal Quality Reviews and Audits

- **Independence and Objectivity:** Ensure reviews and audits are conducted impartially and without bias.

- **Competence:** Assign qualified personnel with expertise in relevant areas to conduct reviews and audits.

- **Documentation:** Maintain thorough documentation of review and audit processes, findings, and outcomes.

- **Transparency:** Communicate findings, recommendations, and action plans transparently to relevant stakeholders.

- **Continuous Learning:** Use review and audit outcomes as opportunities for learning and improvement.

- **Integration:** Integrate feedback and insights from reviews and audits into organizational planning, decision-making, and quality management processes.

Training and Development

Training and development play crucial roles in enhancing employee skills, knowledge, and capabilities, ultimately contributing to organizational growth and success. Here's a comprehensive overview of training and development strategies:

Training

Training focuses on equipping employees with specific skills and competencies required to perform their current roles effectively. It typically includes:

1. **Needs Assessment:**

   - Conduct a thorough analysis to identify skill gaps, training needs, and developmental opportunities within the organization.

   - Consider factors such as job requirements, performance evaluations, feedback from supervisors, and industry trends.

2. **Types of Training Programs:**

   - **Onboarding and Orientation:** Introduce new employees to the organization's culture, policies, procedures, and job responsibilities.

- ○ **Technical Skills Training:** Provide training on specific tools, software, equipment, or technical processes relevant to job functions.

- ○ **Soft Skills Development:** Offer training on interpersonal skills, communication, teamwork, leadership, time management, and problem-solving.

- ○ **Compliance and Regulatory Training:** Ensure employees understand and comply with legal and regulatory requirements specific to their roles.

- ○ **Managerial and Leadership Development:** Train supervisors and managers on leadership principles, performance management, conflict resolution, and decision-making.

3. **Training Methods:**

- ○ **Classroom Training:** Instructor-led sessions conducted onsite or offsite, allowing for interactive learning and immediate feedback.

- ○ **Online Learning (E-Learning):** Utilize digital platforms and courses for self-paced learning, accessible anytime and anywhere.

- ○ **Workshops and Seminars:** Conduct hands-on workshops and seminars to develop practical skills and knowledge.

- ○ **On-the-Job Training (OJT):** Pair employees with experienced mentors or coaches to learn through practical experience and observation.

- **Simulation and Role-Playing:** Create simulated environments or scenarios to practice skills and decision-making in a safe setting.

4. **Evaluation and Feedback:**

- Assess the effectiveness of training programs through pre – and post-training evaluations, quizzes, tests, and feedback surveys.

- Use feedback to make adjustments, improve training content, and address areas of concern or confusion.

Development

Development focuses on preparing employees for future roles and responsibilities within the organization. It includes:

1. **Career Development:**

- Create pathways and opportunities for employees to advance within the organization through promotions, lateral moves, or special projects.

- Offer career counseling, mentorship programs, and development plans tailored to individual aspirations and goals.

2. **Leadership Development:**

- Identify high-potential employees and invest in leadership development programs to cultivate future leaders.

- Provide training in strategic thinking, decision-making, team building, and change management.

3. **Continuous Learning:**

   - Foster a culture of continuous learning and professional growth through ongoing training, seminars, workshops, and self-directed learning.

   - Encourage employees to pursue certifications, attend industry conferences, and participate in communities of practice.

4. **Succession Planning:**

   - Develop succession plans to ensure a smooth transition of key roles and responsibilities within the organization.

   - Identify and groom potential successors through targeted development initiatives and cross-functional experiences.

Best Practices for Training and Development

- **Alignment with Business Goals:** Ensure training and development initiatives align with organizational objectives and strategic priorities.

- **Customization:** Tailor training programs to meet the unique needs and learning styles of employees.

- **Engagement and Participation:** Promote active participation and engagement through interactive activities, case studies, and real-world applications.

- **Measurement of Effectiveness:** Establish metrics and Key Performance Indicators (KPIs) to evaluate the impact of training and development efforts on employee performance and organizational outcomes.

- **Feedback and Continuous Improvement:** Solicit feedback from participants and stakeholders to continuously improve training content, delivery methods, and overall effectiveness.

- **Support from Leadership:** Gain commitment and support from senior management to prioritize and invest in training and development initiatives.

6.2.1 Ongoing Training Programs

Ongoing training programs are essential for maintaining and enhancing employee skills, knowledge, and performance over time. These programs help employees stay current with industry trends, technology advancements, and organizational changes. Here's a detailed look at how ongoing training programs can be structured and implemented effectively:

Structuring Ongoing Training Programs

1. **Needs Assessment and Planning:**

   - Conduct regular needs assessments to identify emerging skill gaps, changing job requirements, and developmental opportunities within the organization.

   - Align training objectives with organizational goals and strategic priorities.

2. **Program Design:**

   o Develop a comprehensive training plan that outlines the scope, objectives, target audience, and timeline for ongoing training initiatives.

   o Include a mix of training methods and formats to accommodate diverse learning styles and preferences.

3. **Training Delivery Methods:**

   o **E-Learning and Online Courses:** Utilize digital platforms and learning management systems (LMS) to offer self-paced online courses and modules.

   o **Instructor-Led Training (ILT):** Conduct scheduled classroom sessions, workshops, or seminars led by subject matter experts or external trainers.

   o **Blended Learning Approaches:** Combine online learning with face-to-face interactions, virtual classrooms, or webinars to maximize engagement and flexibility.

   o **Microlearning:** Deliver short, focused learning modules or bite-sized content that employees can access on-demand.

4. **Topics and Content:**

   o **Technical Skills Development:** Provide training on new technologies, software updates, tools, and technical processes relevant to job roles.

- ○ **Soft Skills Enhancement:** Offer workshops and seminars on communication, leadership, teamwork, time management, and customer service.
- ○ **Industry Trends and Best Practices:** Keep employees informed about industry trends, regulatory changes, and emerging best practices through specialized training sessions.

5. **Certifications and Credentials:**

- ○ Support employees in obtaining industry certifications, licenses, or credentials that enhance their professional qualifications and credibility.
- ○ Offer reimbursement or sponsorship for certification exams and continuing education credits.

Implementing Ongoing Training Programs

1. **Promote a Learning Culture:**

- ○ Foster a culture that values continuous learning, professional growth, and skill development.
- ○ Encourage managers and leaders to actively support and participate in ongoing training initiatives.

2. **Regular Communication:**

- ○ Communicate upcoming training opportunities, schedules, and registration details through internal channels, such as newsletters, intranet portals, and email updates.
- ○ Highlight the benefits and relevance of training programs to encourage employee participation.

3. **Feedback and Evaluation:**

   o Solicit feedback from participants to assess the effectiveness, relevance, and satisfaction with ongoing training programs.

   o Use evaluation metrics, surveys, and post-training assessments to measure learning outcomes and identify areas for improvement.

4. **Continuous Improvement:**

   o Analyze training effectiveness data and participant feedback to refine training content, delivery methods, and program logistics.

   o Incorporate lessons learned and emerging trends into future training plans and curriculum updates.

5. **Resource Allocation:**

   o Allocate adequate resources, including budgetary provisions, time, and technological support, to facilitate ongoing training initiatives.

   o Leverage internal expertise and external partnerships to enhance training quality and relevance.

Benefits of Ongoing Training Programs

- **Enhanced Employee Performance:** Continuously updated skills and knowledge improve job performance and productivity.

- **Employee Engagement and Satisfaction:** Investing in employee development demonstrates organizational commitment and fosters loyalty.

- **Adaptability and Innovation:** Employees equipped with current knowledge and skills can adapt to change more effectively and contribute to innovation.

- **Talent Retention:** Professional growth opportunities through ongoing training programs can help retain top talent within the organization.

Encouraging Professional Development

Encouraging professional development among employees is crucial for nurturing growth, improving job satisfaction, and retaining talent within an organization. Here's a step by step procedure.

1. Create a Culture of Learning and Growth

- **Leadership Support:** Ensure that senior leaders actively endorse and participate in professional development initiatives. Their support sets a positive tone and emphasizes the importance of continuous learning.

- **Promote Awareness:** Regularly communicate the value of professional development to employees. Highlight how ongoing learning contributes to personal career advancement and organizational success.

- **Allocate Resources:** Dedicate budgetary allocations and time allowances for training, courses, certifications, workshops, and conferences related to professional development.

2. Provide Clear Pathways for Advancement

- **Career Planning:** Offer career development discussions and resources to help employees map out their career paths within the organization. This can include mentoring, coaching, and succession planning.

- **Goal Setting:** Encourage employees to set professional development goals aligned with their career aspirations and organizational objectives. These goals should be specific, measurable, achievable, relevant, and time-bound (SMART).

3. Offer a Variety of Development Opportunities

- **Training Programs:** Provide access to both internal and external training programs that cover technical skills, soft skills (e.g., communication, leadership), industry-specific knowledge, and management training.

- **Certifications and Credentials:** Support employees in obtaining relevant certifications and credentials that enhance their expertise and credibility in their field.

- **Cross-functional Experiences:** Facilitate opportunities for employees to work on cross-functional teams, projects, or job rotations to gain new skills and perspectives.

4. Support Continuous Learning

- **Learning Resources:** Provide access to learning resources such as online courses, e-learning platforms, libraries, and industry publications. Consider subscriptions to educational platforms or digital libraries.

- **Skill Development Programs:** Implement workshops, seminars, lunch-and-learns, and webinars on topics of interest and relevance to employees' professional growth.

5. Recognize and Reward Development Efforts

- **Performance Reviews:** Incorporate discussions on professional development progress and achievements into regular performance reviews. Acknowledge and celebrate employees who demonstrate commitment to their growth.

- **Incentives and Benefits:** Consider offering incentives such as bonuses, promotions, or salary increases tied to achieving professional development milestones or acquiring new skills.

6. Create a Supportive Learning Environment

- **Feedback and Mentorship:** Encourage feedback from managers, peers, and mentors to help employees identify strengths, areas for improvement, and opportunities for growth.

- **Peer Learning Networks:** Facilitate peer-to-peer learning through networking events, community groups, or forums where employees can share knowledge and best practices.

7. Measure Impact and Adjust Strategies

- **Evaluation Metrics:** Establish metrics to measure the impact of professional development initiatives on employee performance, engagement, and retention.

- **Feedback Loops:** Gather feedback from employees on the effectiveness of development programs and use this input to refine and improve offerings over time.

Benefits of Encouraging Professional Development

- **Increased Engagement:** Employees feel valued and motivated when given opportunities to learn and grow professionally within the organization.

- **Enhanced Skills and Performance:** Continuous learning helps employees stay current with industry trends and improve their job performance.

- **Talent Retention:** Investing in employees' professional growth increases job satisfaction and reduces turnover by demonstrating a commitment to their long-term success.

- **Innovation and Adaptability:** Employees with diverse skill sets and knowledge contribute to innovation and help organizations adapt to changing market dynamics.

Encouraging professional development in a 24x7 IT service desk team is crucial for maintaining high performance, employee satisfaction, and providing excellent service to customers. Here are some strategies you can implement:

1. Training Programs

- **Regular Training Sessions:** Conduct regular training sessions on new technologies, tools, and processes.

- **Cross-Training:** Encourage team members to learn different roles within the service desk to increase flexibility and understanding.

- **Certification Support:** Provide support for relevant certifications, including financial assistance and time off for studying.

2. Mentoring and Coaching

- **Mentorship Programs:** Pair experienced staff with newer employees to guide their development.
- **Coaching Sessions:** Regular one-on-one coaching sessions to discuss career goals and development plans.

3. Career Pathing

- **Clear Career Paths:** Define clear career progression paths within the organization.
- **Internal Promotions:** Promote from within whenever possible to motivate employees to develop their skills.

4. Performance Feedback

- **Regular Reviews:** Conduct regular performance reviews to provide constructive feedback.
- **Recognition Programs:** Recognize and reward employees for exceptional performance and professional development achievements.

5. Learning Culture

- **Encourage Learning:** Foster a culture where continuous learning is encouraged and supported.
- **Learning Resources:** Provide access to online courses, books, and other learning materials.

6. Work-Life Balance

- **Flexible Scheduling:** Offer flexible scheduling to accommodate learning and development activities.

- **Time Management:** Teach effective time management to balance professional development with work duties.

7. Engagement and Motivation

- **Engage Employees:** Involve employees in decision-making processes and encourage their input on development initiatives.

- **Incentive Programs:** Implement incentive programs for employees who actively pursue professional development.

8. Technological Support

- **Access to Tools:** Ensure employees have access to the latest tools and technologies to stay current.

- **Sandbox Environments:** Provide environments where employees can experiment with new technologies without affecting production.

9. Community and Networking

- **Professional Communities:** Encourage participation in professional communities and industry events.

- **Networking Opportunities:** Provide opportunities for networking with other professionals in the field.

10. Measure and Adjust

- **Track Progress:** Regularly measure the effectiveness of professional development programs and adjust as needed.

- **Feedback Mechanisms:** Implement feedback mechanisms to understand the needs and preferences of your team regarding professional development.

Implementing these strategies can help create a motivated, skilled, and adaptable IT service desk team capable of meeting the demands of a 24x7 operation.

Chapter Summary – Mindmap

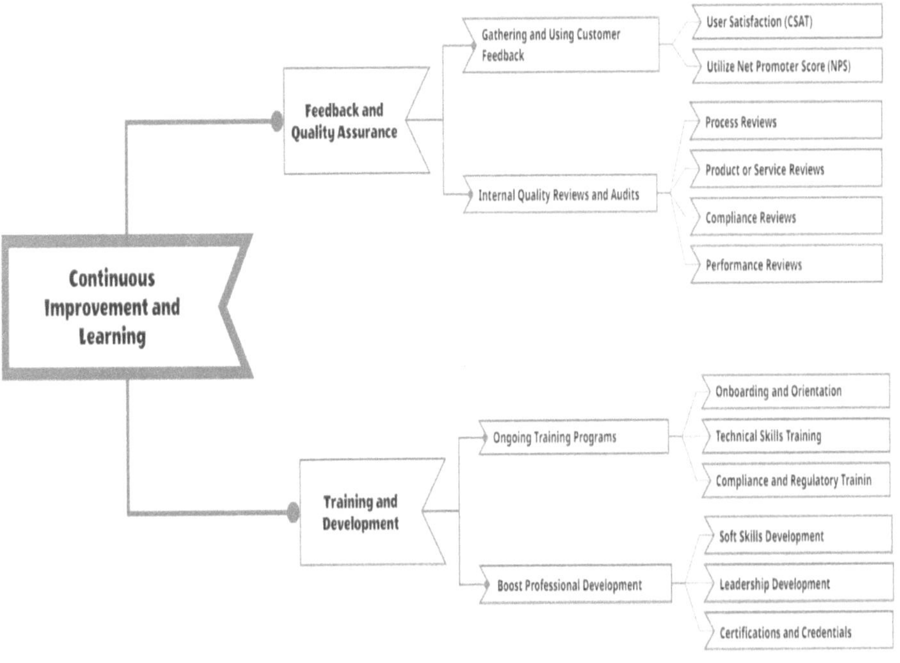

Chapter 7

Managing a 24x7 Service Desk

Managing a 24x7 service desk involves ensuring continuous, high-quality support while maintaining team morale and efficiency. Key strategies include implementing rotating shifts to avoid burnout, providing comprehensive training and cross-training to enhance flexibility, and leveraging automation to handle routine tasks. Effective communication and documentation are crucial for seamless handovers between shifts. Regular performance reviews, recognition programs, and career development opportunities keep staff motivated. Additionally, maintaining a robust incident management system ensures quick resolution of issues, and encouraging a culture of continuous improvement helps the team adapt to evolving challenges and technologies.

7.1   Challenges of 24x7 Operations

Managing a 24x7 operation presents several unique challenges, including:

1. **Staffing and Scheduling** – Finding skilled and experienced staff who are flexible and adaptable to the needs of the organization and its projects can be very challenging.

2. **Consistency and Quality** – Maintaining high-quality service consistently across all shifts from the entire team can also be a significant challenge.

3. **Communication** – Effective communication between shifts and Service Desk Agents (SDAs) is crucial to achieving the overall goals of the service or product.

4. **Employee Morale and Retention** – Keeping the team motivated and satisfied with their work is a significant challenge.

5. **Technology and Tools** – Finding the right tools and technologies that align with the organization's needs and constraints for delivering support services is a significant challenge.

7.1.1 Staffing and Scheduling best practices.

Staffing and scheduling for a 24x7 service desk are critical components to ensure continuous, efficient, and high-quality service. Here are some best practices and strategies:

1. Shift Patterns

- **Rotating Shifts:** Implement rotational shift patterns to distribute night and weekend work uniformly among all staff members.
- **Fixed Shifts:** Offer fixed shifts for team members who prefer consistent hours, which can boost morale and bring stability in the team.

2. Coverage

- **Shift Overlaps:** Schedule overlap timings between shifts to ensure smooth handovers and continuity of support.

- **Peak Times:** Identify customer peak business hours and allocate more staff during these periods to manage additional workload.

3. Overload Management

- **Between the shifts:** Ensure adequate time to rest between shifts to prevent exhaustion.

- **Shorter Night Shifts:** Consider planning shorter night shifts to reduce the impact on employees' health and well-being.

4. Flexibility

- **Flexible Scheduling:** Offer flexible scheduling options to accommodate employees' personal needs and preferences.

- **Shift Swaps:** Allow employees to swap shifts with each other to increase flexibility and satisfaction.

5. Overtime and Backup Plans

- **Overtime Management:** Monitor and manage overtime to avoid burnouts in the team.

- **Backup Staff:** Plan and schedule the shifts considering a backup plan for emergencies and sudden unplanned leaves.

6. Technology and Tools

- **Scheduling Software:** Scheduling software like 'Shiftboard' 'When I work', 'Deputy', etc. can be considered for efficient and fair schedules, track hours, and manage changes.

- **Real-Time Monitoring:** Tools can be used to monitor real-time workload and adjust staffing as needed.

7. Cross-Training

- **Skill Diversification:** Cross-skilling staffs to handle different roles, enhancing flexibility and coverage options.

- **Rotation:** Regularly rotate employees through different tasks and responsibilities to keep skills sharp and improve job satisfaction.

8.Communication

- **Clear Policies:** Establish and communicate clear shift scheduling policies and procedures.

- **Feedback Channels:** Provide channels for employees to give feedback on scheduling and workload, and work on continuous improvement.

9. Work-Life Balance

- **Time-Off Policies:** Ensure fair and transparent policies for time off, including weekly offs, vacations and personal days.

- **Support Systems:** Provide support for employees dealing with the challenges of irregular hours, such as medical assistance, counseling, or wellness programs.

10. Performance Monitoring

- **Regular Reviews:** Conduct regular performance reviews to ensure that staffing levels and schedules meet operational needs.

- **Adjustments:** Be prepared to make adjustments based on performance data, employee feedback, and changing business needs.

7.1.2 Maintaining Consistency and Quality

Maintaining consistency and quality in a 24x7 service desk environment is crucial for providing reliable support and ensuring customer satisfaction. Here are some key strategies:

1. Standardized Processes

- **Documented Procedures:** Design and maintain comprehensive, documented procedures for common tasks, requests, and incidents.

- **Process Adherence:** Make sure all team members adhere to standardized processes to maintain uniform service quality.

2. Training and Development

- **Regular Training:** Consciously plan ongoing training to keep staff updated on the latest tools, technologies, and best practices.

- **Cross-Training:** Train employees in multiple skills, roles and responsibilities to ensure flexibility and comprehensive service.

3. Communication

- **Effective Handovers:** Develop and establish structured handover processes between shifts to ensure smooth transitions and continuity.

- **Communication Tools:** Use robust communication tools (e.g., chat platforms, ticketing systems) to facilitate information sharing among team members.

4. Quality Assurance

- **Performance Monitoring:** Regularly monitor performance metrics and KPIs to assess and improve service quality.

- **Quality Reviews:** Conduct regular quality reviews and audits of tickets and interactions to identify areas for improvement.

5. Feedback Mechanisms

- **Customer Feedback:** Regularly collect and analyze customer feedback to identify strengths and areas for improvement.

- **Internal Feedback:** Encourage internal feedback from team members to continuously refine processes and address issues.

6. Knowledge Management

- **Knowledge Base:** Maintain a comprehensive and up-to-date knowledge base accessible to all team members.

- **Documentation Standards:** Ensure all documentation is clear, concise, and regularly updated maintaining the uniformity.

7. Performance Metrics

- **KPIs:** Define and track key performance indicators (KPIs) such as response time, resolution time, customer satisfaction, ticket trend, ticket backlog.

- **Regular Reporting:** Generate regular reports to analyze performance trends and make appropriate decisions based on the data points.

8. Continuous Improvement

- **Root Cause Analysis:** Conduct root cause analysis for recurring issues to prevent future occurrences.

- **Process Improvement:** Regularly review and refine processes based on feedback and performance data analysis.

9. Team Collaboration

- **Collaborative Culture:** Establish and encourage a culture of collaboration and knowledge sharing among team members.

- **Team Meetings:** Establish regular team meetings to discuss challenges, share insights, and align on goals.

10. Technology and Tools

- **Automation:** Use automation tools to handle routine tasks and ensure consistent execution to make team more productive.

- **Integrated Systems:** Ensure all systems and tools are integrated to provide a seamless workflow and reduce manual errors.

11. Leadership and Support

- **Strong Leadership:** Establish strong leadership layer to guide the team and maintain high standards.

- **Support Systems:** Design support systems such as mentoring and coaching to help employees perform at their best.

7.2 Strategies for Effective 24x7 Management

Effective management of a 24x7 service desk requires a combination of strategic planning, efficient processes, and a focus on employee well-being. Here are some key strategies:

1. Comprehensive Staffing and Scheduling

- **Shift Rotation:** Implement fair and balanced rotating shifts to distribute workload evenly and prevent burnout.

- **Shift Overlaps:** Schedule overlapping shifts to facilitate smooth handovers and ensure continuous coverage.

- **Flexibility:** Offer flexible scheduling options to accommodate employees' personal needs and improve work-life balance.

2. Robust Training and Development

- **Initial Training:** Provide comprehensive onboarding training for new hires to ensure they are well-prepared to handle the shifts independently.

- **Ongoing Training:** Regularly update training programs to keep staff up-to date with the latest tools, technologies, and best practices.

- **Cross-Skill Training:** Cross-skill training employees in multiple roles to increase flexibility, learning and job satisfaction.

3. Effective Communication

- **Clear Policies:** Establish clear communication policies and procedures for shift handovers and daily operations.

- **Collaboration Tools:** Utilize collaboration tools such as instant messaging, video conferencing, and ticketing systems to facilitate communication.

- **Regular Meetings:** Hold regular team meetings to discuss updates, challenges, and improvements.

4. Performance Monitoring and Quality Assurance

- **KPIs and Metrics:** Define and track key performance indicators (KPIs) such as response tazztimes, resolution rates, and customer satisfaction.

- **Quality Audits:** Conduct regular quality audits to ensure adherence to standards and identify areas for improvement.

- **Feedback Loop:** Implement a feedback loop with customers and team members to continuously improve service quality.

5. Incident Management and Escalation

- **Incident Protocols:** Develop and document clear incident management and escalation protocols.
- **Rapid Response:** Ensure rapid response times to critical incidents regardless of the time of day.
- **Escalation Procedures:** Establish clear escalation paths for handling complex or high-priority issues.

6. Resource Allocation and Utilization

- **Workload Analysis:** Analyze workload patterns to allocate resources efficiently and manage peak business hours effectively.
- **Automation:** Implement automation for routine tasks to free up staff for more complex issues and improve efficiency.
- **Backup Plans:** Maintain a pool of backup staff to cover unexpected absences or spike in the ticket volume.

7. Employee Well-being and Morale

- **Support Systems:** Provide support systems such as counseling, wellness programs, and stress management resources.
- **Recognition and Rewards:** Recognize and reward exceptional performance and contributions to maintain high morale.
- **Engagement Activities:** Organize team building and engagement activities like team lunch and outings to create positive work environment.

8. Technology and Tools

- **Reliable Infrastructure:** Ensure all technological tools and systems are reliable and available around the clock.

- **Continuous Improvement:** Regularly review and update technology to keep pace with industry advancements and operational needs.

9. Continuous Improvement

- **Root Cause Analysis:** Conduct root cause analysis for recurring issues to prevent future occurrences.

- **Process Optimization:** Continuously review and optimize processes based on feedback and performance data.

- **Innovation:** Encourage innovation and experimentation to find new ways to improve efficiency and service quality.

10. Leadership and Management Support

- **Strong Leadership:** Provide strong leadership to guide the team, set clear goals, and maintain high standards.

- **Manager Accessibility:** Ensure managers are accessible and supportive, especially during off-hours when challenges may arise.

7.2.1 Shift Handover Processes

Effective shift handover processes are crucial for maintaining consistency, quality, and continuity in a 24x7 service desk environment. Here are some best practices for implementing and managing shift handovers:

1. Structured Handover Protocols

- **Standardized Format:** Develop a standardized handover format or checklist to ensure all critical information are covered and communicated effectively.

- **Documentation:** Document all handover procedures and ensure they are easily accessible to all team members.

2. Key Information Sharing

- **Current Status:** Provide an overview of the status of ongoing issues, projects, and any significant events during the shift.

- **Pending Tasks:** List all pending tasks and any actions required by the incoming shift.

- **Critical Incidents:** Highlight any critical incidents or escalations, including their current status and any follow-up actions needed.

3. Effective Communication Tools

- **Logs and Reports:** Maintain detailed logs and shift reports that can be reviewed by incoming staff.

- **Collaboration Platforms:** Use collaboration tools such as shared documents, ticketing systems, and chat platforms to facilitate real-time information sharing.

4. Overlap and Transition Time

- **Shift Overlap:** Schedule a brief overlap period between shifts to allow for direct communication and questions.

- **Face-to-Face Handover:** Whenever possible, conduct face-to-face or virtual handover meetings to ensure clarity and address any immediate concerns.

5. Critical Incident Briefings

- **Incident Summaries:** Provide summaries of any incidents that occurred during the shift, including actions taken and current status.

- **Next Steps:** Outline the next steps required to resolve ongoing incidents or issues.

6. Verification and Acknowledgment

- **Checklists:** Use checklists to ensure all important information has been communicated and acknowledged by the incoming staff.

- **Confirmation:** Require incoming staff to confirm they have received and understood the handover information.

7. Continuous Improvement

- **Feedback:** Gather feedback from staff on the handover process to identify areas for improvement.

- **Regular Reviews:** Regularly review and update handover procedures based on feedback and evolving needs.

8. Training and Awareness

- **Handover Training:** Provide training on effective handover practices and the importance of thorough communication.

- **Awareness Campaigns:** Conduct awareness campaigns to reinforce the importance of proper handover processes.

9. Monitoring and Auditing

- **Spot Checks:** Conduct regular spot checks and audits of handover logs and reports to ensure compliance with established procedures.

- **Performance Metrics:** Track performance metrics related to handover quality and address any issues promptly.

10. Technology Integration

- **Unified Systems:** Use integrated systems that allow seamless transfer of information between shifts.

- **Automated Alerts:** Implement automated alerts and notifications to remind staff of handover times and critical tasks.

By implementing these practices, you can ensure that shift handovers in your 24x7 service desk are smooth, comprehensive, and effective, thereby maintaining service continuity and quality.

7.2.2 Using Automation and Tools

Automation and advanced tools can significantly enhance the effectiveness of managing a 24x7 service desk. Here are strategies for leveraging these technologies:

1. Incident and Ticket Management

- **Automated Ticket Routing:** Use automation to route tickets to the appropriate team or individual based on predefined rules and criteria.

- **Ticket Prioritization:** Implement automated systems to prioritize tickets based on urgency, impact, and predefined SLAs (Service Level Agreements).

2. Monitoring and Alerting

- **Real-Time Monitoring:** Deploy monitoring tools to continuously track system performance, network health, and application availability.

- **Automated Alerts:** Set up automated alerts to notify relevant staff about critical incidents, performance issues, or security breaches.

3. Self-Service Portals

- **Knowledge Base:** Create a comprehensive, searchable knowledge base that customers and employees can access for self-help.

- **Automated Responses:** Implement chatbots and virtual assistants to provide instant responses to common queries and issues.

4. Performance Monitoring and Reporting

- **Dashboards:** Use real-time dashboards to monitor key performance indicators (KPIs) and track the status of ongoing issues.

- **Automated Reports:** Generate automated reports on performance metrics, incident trends, and team productivity.

6. Shift Management

- **Scheduling Tools:** Utilize advanced scheduling tools to create and manage shift rosters, ensuring optimal coverage and flexibility.

- **Handover Logs:** Implement digital handover logs to document and track shift changes, ensuring smooth transitions and continuity.

7. Communication and Collaboration

- **Unified Communication Platforms:** Adopt unified communication platforms that integrate chat, email, video conferencing, and ticketing systems for seamless collaboration.

- **Knowledge Sharing:** Use collaboration tools to facilitate knowledge sharing and ensure all team members have access to the latest information and updates.

8. Continuous Improvement

- **Feedback Mechanisms:** Implement automated feedback mechanisms to collect customer and employee feedback after issue resolution.

- **Analytics Tools:** Use analytics tools to identify patterns, trends, and areas for improvement in service delivery.

Benefits of Using Automation and Tools

- **Increased Efficiency:** Automation reduces manual effort, allowing staff to focus on higher-value tasks.

- **Consistency and Accuracy:** Automated processes ensure consistency and accuracy in handling routine tasks and incidents.

- **Faster Response Times:** Automation enables faster response and resolution times, improving customer satisfaction.

- **Enhanced Visibility:** Real-time monitoring and reporting tools provide enhanced visibility into operations, facilitating better decision-making.

- **Cost Savings:** Reducing manual work and streamlining processes can lead to significant cost savings over time.

Chapter Summary – Mindmap

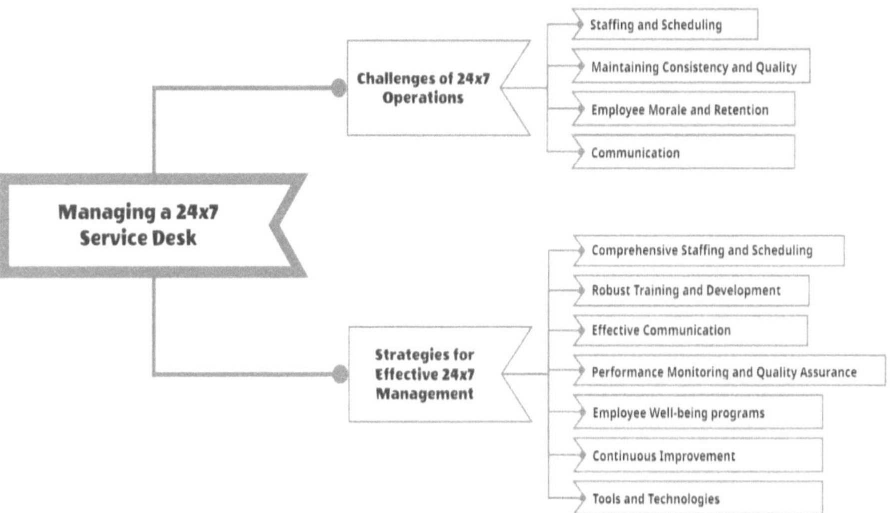

Chapter 8

Case Studies and Real-World Examples

8.1 Success Stories

The below success stories demonstrate how 24x7 IT service desks can achieve remarkable results by implementing best practices, leveraging technology, and prioritizing customer and employee needs.

8.1.1 Examples of Effective Service Desks

Success stories of 24x7 IT service desks highlight the impact of effective management strategies, advanced tools, and dedicated teams in delivering exceptional support. Here are a few notable examples:

1. Global Technology Company

Challenge: The company faced high volumes of support tickets and inconsistent service quality across different time zones.

Solution:

- Implemented a 24x7 service desk with rotating shifts and automated ticket routing.

- Deployed a comprehensive knowledge base and self-service portal.

- Used real-time monitoring and automated alerts for proactive issue management.

Outcome:

- Reduced average ticket resolution time by 40%.

- Achieved a 95% customer satisfaction rate.

- Improved consistency in service quality across all regions.

2. Financial Services Firm

Challenge: The firm needed to ensure uninterrupted support for critical financial applications and data security.

Solution:

- Established a 24x7 service desk with specialized teams for critical applications.

- Integrated advanced security monitoring tools and automated incident response.

- Implemented robust shift handover processes and continuous training programs.

Outcome:

- Maintained 99.99% uptime for critical applications.

- Reduced security incident response time by 50%.

- Enhanced employee expertise and preparedness through continuous training.

3. Healthcare Organization

Challenge: The organization required 24x7 support to ensure the availability of essential healthcare systems and patient data.

Solution:

- Set up a 24x7 service desk with dedicated support for healthcare applications.

- Implemented automated monitoring and alerting for system performance and data integrity.

- Provided remote support tools and a centralized knowledge base for quick issue resolution.

Outcome:

- Improved system availability to 99.98%.

- Increased first-call resolution rate to 85%.

- Received positive feedback from healthcare professionals on support quality.

4. E-commerce Giant

Challenge: The e-commerce company experienced high demand for customer support during peak shopping seasons and needed to manage scalability.

Solution:

- Scaled the 24x7 service desk with flexible staffing and automated ticket management during peak periods.

- Used AI-driven chatbots for handling common customer queries and issues.

- Implemented performance monitoring and real-time dashboards for quick decision-making.

Outcome:

- Successfully managed a 200% increase in support tickets during peak seasons.

- Reduced customer query resolution time by 35%.

- Achieved a 4.8/5 customer satisfaction rating during peak periods.

5. Telecommunications Provider

Challenge: The provider needed to ensure continuous support for network operations and customer services across multiple regions.

Solution:

- Established a global 24x7 service desk with regional teams for localized support.

- Deployed advanced network monitoring tools and automated incident management.

- Provided extensive training and career development programs for staff.

Outcome:

- Enhanced network reliability with a 99.97% uptime.

- Improved incident resolution time by 45%.

- Increased employee retention rate due to strong career development opportunities.

Key Takeaways

- **Strategic Staffing:** Implementing rotating shifts, specialized teams, and flexible staffing models can effectively manage high support volumes and maintain service quality.

- **Automation:** Leveraging automation for ticket management, monitoring, and incident response significantly improves efficiency and reduces response times.

- **Continuous Training:** Ongoing training and development ensure that staff are well-prepared to handle complex issues and adapt to new technologies.

- **Proactive Monitoring:** Real-time monitoring and automated alerts enable proactive issue management, reducing downtime and enhancing system reliability.

- **Customer Satisfaction:** A focus on customer satisfaction through effective support processes, self-service options, and feedback mechanisms leads to high satisfaction rates.

- **Incident Management case study**

It was a typical Tuesday morning at Tech Solutions, a global IT service provider, when suddenly, the company's email server went down. This incident disrupted communication across all departments, affecting client interactions and internal operations. The clock was ticking, and the incident management team had to act fast.

Case Study: Incident Management at ABCD Solutions

Background

ABCD Solutions, an IT services provider headquartered in Bengaluru, manages the IT infrastructure of Shakti Industries, a leading manufacturing company based in Pune. The partnership ensures 24/7 IT support for Shakti's critical business operations, including their ERP system, *Samagra ERP*.

Incident Overview

On a busy Monday morning, *Samagra ERP* became unresponsive, halting production at Shakti Industries' Pune plant. The incident required immediate action to prevent financial losses.

Incident Timeline with Communications

9:15 AM: Initial Report

Phone Call:

- **Deepak Joshi** (IT Manager, Shakti Industries) called the ABCD service desk.

    - **Deepak:** "Priya, our *Samagra ERP* is down, and production has completely stopped. We need urgent help."

    - **Priya Sharma** (Service Desk Analyst): "Understood, Deepak. I'll escalate this as a Priority 1 incident immediately."

Email Notification:

- **Subject:** P1 Incident Logged: *Samagra ERP* Downtime
- **From:** Priya Sharma
- **To:** Ravi Kumar (Incident Manager), Anil Mehta (Network Specialist), Sneha Iyer (Application Support)
- **CC:** Karthik Reddy (Account Manager), Deepak Joshi
- **Content:**

```
Hello Team,

A Priority 1 incident has been reported by
Shakti Industries. Their *Samagra ERP* system
is unresponsive, halting production at their
Pune plant.

Initial Details:

- Client: Shakti Industries
- Issue: ERP System Down
- Impact: Entire production line
- Reported by: Deepak Joshi (IT Manager)

Please join the war room immediately to resolve
this issue.

War Room Link: [Join Here]

Regards,
Priya Sharma
Service Desk Analyst
```

9:30 AM: War Room Discussion

Participants: Ravi Kumar, Anil Mehta, Sneha Iyer, Priya Sharma

- **Ravi:** "Anil, please check the network connectivity between Shakti's Pune plant and our Mumbai data center."
- **Anil:** "On it, Ravi. I'll run a trace route and check the logs."
- **Sneha:** "I'll review the application logs on the ERP server."

10:15 AM: Updates

Email Notification:

- **Subject:** Incident Update: Root Cause Investigation Underway
- **From:** Ravi Kumar
- **To:** Deepak Joshi, Karthik Reddy
- **Content:**

```
Hello,

The team is actively investigating the root
cause of the ERP downtime.

Current Findings:

- Application logs: No errors detected.
- Network: High latency observed between Pune
  plant and Mumbai data center.

Next Steps:

- Anil is diagnosing the network issue.
```

```
- Sneha is running a deeper analysis of the
  application logs.
```

```
We'll provide the next update in 30 minutes.
```

```
Regards,
Ravi Kumar
Incident Manager
```

11:00 AM: Root Cause Identified

Phone Call:

- **Anil:** "Ravi, I've identified the issue. A misconfiguration in the Pune router, updated during last night's maintenance window, is causing the VPN latency."

- **Ravi:** "Good work, Anil. Fix the configuration remotely and inform Sneha to verify the ERP system after the change."

11:30 AM: Resolution

Email Notification:

- **Subject:** Incident Resolved: *Samagra ERP* Restored

- **From:** Ravi Kumar

- **To:** Deepak Joshi, Karthik Reddy

- **Content:**

```
Hello,

The *Samagra ERP* issue has been resolved.
```

Root Cause:

- A misconfigured router at the Pune plant caused VPN latency, making the ERP system unresponsive.

Actions Taken:

- Router configuration corrected.
- ERP system functionality verified.

We recommend a review of the change management process to avoid such issues in the future.

Please confirm that operations have resumed.

Regards,
Ravi Kumar
Incident Manager

Response Email:

- **From:** Deepak Joshi

- **To:** Ravi Kumar

- **Content:**

Thank you, Ravi.

The ERP system is now operational, and production has resumed. We appreciate the quick resolution.

Regards,
Deepak Joshi
IT Manager, Shakti Industries

Post-Incident Review

Meeting Notes:

1. **Key Findings:**

   - Network configuration changes caused the incident.

   - No prior impact analysis was conducted.

2. **Recommendations:**

   - Enhance monitoring tools for real-time detection of latency issues.

   - Implement stricter change management protocols.

Follow-Up Email:

- **Subject:** Post-Incident Review: Action Items

- **From:** Ravi Kumar

- **To:** Team ABCD Tech Solution

- **CC:** Deepak Joshi

- **Content:**

```
Hello Team,

Following the post-incident review, here are
the action items:

1. Update monitoring tools to include VPN
   latency alerts.
2. Revise change management protocols to include
   impact analysis.
```

```
Let's aim to complete these tasks by the end
of the month.

Regards,
Ravi Kumar
Incident Manager
```

Outcome

Shakti Industries commended ABCD Tech for their swift response and professional handling of the incident. The incident highlighted key areas for improvement, leading to enhanced processes and a stronger client relationship.

Case Study: Problem Management at ABCD Solutions

Background

ABCD Solutions, a Bengaluru-based IT services company, provides 24/7 IT infrastructure support to Akshay Foods, a major food processing company in Hyderabad. Akshay Foods reported recurring outages of their warehouse management system (*Dharini WMS*), causing delays in logistics and impacting delivery timelines.

Incident Overview

Over two weeks, three separate incidents of *Dharini WMS* downtime were reported. While incidents were resolved temporarily, the recurring nature required a deeper analysis to prevent future occurrences.

Problem Management Initiation

Step 1: Problem Identification

Email Notification (Trigger):

- **Subject:** Recurring WMS Downtime – Problem Management Initiation

- **From:** Ravi Kumar (Problem Manager)

- **To:** Akshay Foods IT Team, ABCD Technical Leads

- **CC:** Karthik Reddy (Account Manager), Priya Sharma (Service Desk Lead)

- **Content:**

```
Hello Team,

Over the past two weeks, Akshay Foods has faced
recurring downtime with the *Dharini WMS*.
To address this, we are initiating a Problem
Management process to identify the root cause
and implement a permanent solution.

Problem Details:

- Service Affected: Dharini WMS
- Occurrences: 3 (Dates: 10th, 15th, and 20th
  November 2024)
- Temporary Fix: Restarting the application
  server

Please join the Problem Management kickoff
meeting tomorrow at 10:00 AM IST.

Meeting Link: [Join Here]

Regards,
Ravi Kumar
Problem Manager
```

Step 2: Problem Analysis

Meeting: Kickoff Discussion

- **Participants:** Ravi Kumar (Problem Manager), Anil Mehta (Network Specialist), Sneha Iyer (Application Support), Priya Sharma (Service Desk Lead), Deepak Joshi (Akshay Foods IT Manager)

- **Key Discussion Points:**

  - Deepak highlighted that the downtime often occurred during peak hours, affecting logistics planning.

  - Sneha shared that during each incident, the *WMS application logs* showed spikes in database query times.

  - Anil confirmed network stability during the reported incidents.

Follow-Up Email:

- **Subject:** Kickoff Summary: Problem Management for WMS Downtime

- **From:** Ravi Kumar

- **To:** All Meeting Participants

- **Content:**

```
Hello Team,

Thank you for joining the kickoff meeting.
```

```
Summary of Observations:

- The issue appears related to database query
  performance.
- Network stability has been ruled out as a
  cause.

Next Steps:

1. Sneha will perform a deep dive into database
   performance metrics.
2. Anil will validate application-to-database
   connectivity for potential bottlenecks.
3. Priya will document all past incidents for
   trend analysis.

Deadline for updates: End of day, 25th November
2024.

Regards,
Ravi Kumar
Problem Manager
```

Step 3: Root Cause Identification

Phone Call:

- **Sneha Iyer to Ravi Kumar:**

  - **Sneha:** "Ravi, I've analyzed the database logs and noticed a pattern. Every downtime coincides with a high volume of bulk upload transactions initiated by warehouse staff."

  - **Ravi:** "That's a solid lead. Let's investigate if the bulk uploads are overwhelming the database resources."

Email Update:

- **Subject:** Update: Root Cause of WMS Downtime Identified

- **From:** Ravi Kumar

- **To:** Akshay Foods IT Team, ABCD Technical Leads

- **Content:**

```
Hello Team,

The root cause of the recurring WMS downtime has
been identified. During peak hours, bulk upload
transactions are overwhelming the database,
causing query performance degradation.

Proposed Actions:

1. Limit bulk uploads to non-peak hours.
2. Optimize database queries to handle large
   transactions more efficiently.
3. Implement additional database indexing to
   improve performance.

Let's discuss the implementation plan in
tomorrow's meeting at 3:00 PM IST.

Regards,
Ravi Kumar
Problem Manager
```

Step 4: Implementation

Meeting: Action Plan Finalization

- **Deepak Joshi:** "We'll instruct warehouse staff to schedule bulk uploads after 8:00 PM."

- **Sneha Iyer:** "I'll work on optimizing the database queries and indexing changes this week."
- **Ravi Kumar:** "Great. Let's monitor performance for two weeks after implementing these changes."

Email Summary:

- **Subject:** Action Plan Finalized: WMS Problem Resolution
- **From:** Ravi Kumar
- **To:** All Stakeholders
- **Content:**

```
Hello Team,

The following actions will be taken to resolve
the WMS downtime issue:

1. Bulk uploads will be scheduled post 8:00 PM
   (Effective immediately).
2. Database query optimization and indexing
   changes will be implemented by Sneha
   (Deadline: 30th November).
3. Performance monitoring will continue for
   two weeks post-implementation.

Please ensure compliance with these measures.

Regards,
Ravi Kumar
Problem Manager
```

Step 5: Verification

Email:

- **Subject:** Monitoring Results: WMS Stability Restored
- **From:** Ravi Kumar
- **To:** Akshay Foods IT Team, ABCD Technical Leads
- **Content:**

```
Hello Team,

Post-implementation monitoring has confirmed
that the WMS system is now stable, with no
downtime reported since the changes were
applied.

Thank you for your cooperation in resolving
this issue.

Regards,
Ravi Kumar
Problem Manager
```

Outcome

The permanent solution eliminated the recurring downtime of *Dharini WMS*, improving logistics efficiency at Akshay Foods. The proactive problem management approach strengthened the partnership between ABCD solutions and Akshay Foods.

Case Study: Request Fulfillment at ABCD Solutions

Background

ABCD Solutions, a Bengaluru-based IT services provider, manages IT operations for Srishti Pharmaceuticals, a pharmaceutical manufacturing company in Ahmedabad. Srishti Pharmaceuticals requested ABCD to provide new laptops for their R&D team to support a critical project. The request needed to be fulfilled within three business days due to strict deadlines.

Request Overview

Request Details:

- **Request ID:** RF-2024-1125
- **Requester:** Pooja Shah, IT Manager, Srishti Pharmaceuticals
- **Requirement:** 10 high-performance laptops for the R&D team.
- **Deadline:** 3 business days (due to project urgency).

Request Timeline with Communications

Day 1: Request Submission

Email from Pooja Shah:

- **Subject:** Request for New Laptops for R&D Team

- **From:** Pooja Shah
- **To:** Priya Sharma (Service Desk Analyst)
- **Content:**

```
Hi Priya,

We urgently need 10 high-performance laptops
for our R&D team to start a critical project.
The laptops should have at least the following
specifications:

—  Processor: Intel Core i7
—  RAM: 16GB
—  Storage: 512GB SSD
—  OS: Windows 11 Pro

Please let me know the earliest possible
delivery date.

Regards,
Pooja Shah
IT Manager, Srishti Pharmaceuticals
```

Acknowledgment Email from Priya Sharma:

- **Subject:** Request Acknowledged: RF-2024-1125
- **From:** Priya Sharma
- **To:** Pooja Shah
- **Content:**

```
Hi Pooja,

Thank you for your request. The request ID is RF-
2024-1125. I'll review the specifications and
```

```
coordinate with the procurement and logistics
teams. I'll update you on the delivery timeline
by the end of the day.

Regards,
Priya Sharma
Service Desk Analyst
```

Internal Email from Priya Sharma to Procurement Team:

- **Subject:** Urgent Laptop Request: RF-2024-1125

- **From:** Priya Sharma

- **To:** Arjun Desai (Procurement Lead), Sneha Iyer (Inventory Manager)

- **Content:**

```
Hi Arjun and Sneha,

We have received an urgent request for 10
laptops with the following specifications:

-  Processor: Intel Core i7
-  RAM: 16GB
-  Storage: 512GB SSD
-  OS: Windows 11 Pro

Please confirm availability or lead time for
procurement. The deadline is 3 business days.

Regards,
Priya Sharma
```

Day 1: Response from Procurement Team

Email from Arjun Desai:

- **Subject:** Re: Urgent Laptop Request: RF-2024-1125
- **From:** Arjun Desai
- **To:** Priya Sharma
- **Content:**

```
Hi Priya,

We currently have 6 laptops in stock that
meet the specifications. For the remaining 4
laptops, I can arrange expedited procurement
through our vendor, TechMart India. The vendor
has confirmed delivery within 2 business days.

Please confirm if we can proceed.

Regards,
Arjun Desai
Procurement Lead
```

Phone Call:

- **Priya Sharma to Pooja Shah**

  - **Priya:** "Hi Pooja, we can deliver 6 laptops from our stock immediately. The remaining 4 will be procured and delivered within two business days. Does that work for your team?"

  - **Pooja:** "Yes, that works. Please proceed with the arrangement."

Confirmation Email from Priya Sharma to Procurement:

- **Subject:** Proceed with Laptop Procurement: RF-2024-1125
- **From:** Priya Sharma
- **To:** Arjun Desai, Sneha Iyer
- **Content:**

```
Hi Arjun,

Please proceed with delivering 6 laptops from
stock and procuring the remaining 4 laptops
through TechMart India. Ensure the delivery of
all laptops within the stipulated deadline.

Regards,
Priya Sharma
```

Day 2: Partial Fulfillment

Delivery Confirmation Email from Sneha Iyer:

- **Subject:** Partial Delivery Confirmation: RF-2024-1125
- **From:** Sneha Iyer
- **To:** Priya Sharma, Pooja Shah
- **Content:**

```
Hi Priya and Pooja,

The first batch of 6 laptops has been delivered
to Srishti Pharmaceuticals' Ahmedabad office.

Regards,
Sneha Iyer
Inventory Manager
```

Acknowledgment Email from Pooja Shah:

- **Subject:** Acknowledgment of Partial Delivery: RF-2024-1125
- **From:** Pooja Shah
- **To:** Priya Sharma
- **Content:**

```
Hi Priya,

Thanks for the update. We've received the 6
laptops and have set them up for the R&D team.
Looking forward to the delivery of the remaining
4 laptops as planned.

Regards,
Pooja Shah
```

Day 3: Completion of Fulfillment

Delivery Notification Email from Arjun Desai:

- **Subject:** Final Delivery Confirmation: RF-2024-1125
- **From:** Arjun Desai
- **To:** Priya Sharma, Sneha Iyer, Pooja Shah
- **Content:**

```
Hi Team,

The remaining 4 laptops have been delivered
to Srishti Pharmaceuticals' Ahmedabad office
today.

Regards,
Arjun Desai
Procurement Lead
```

Acknowledgment Email from Pooja Shah:

- **Subject:** Request Completed: RF-2024-1125
- **From:** Pooja Shah
- **To:** Priya Sharma
- **Content:**

```
Hi Priya,

The remaining laptops have been received. Thank
you and your team for fulfilling this request
within the deadline.

Regards,
Pooja Shah
```

Post-Request Review

Follow-Up Email from Priya Sharma:

- **Subject:** Feedback Request: Laptop Fulfillment – RF-2024-1125
- **From:** Priya Sharma
- **To:** Pooja Shah
- **Content:**

```
Hi Pooja,

Thank you for confirming the receipt of all
laptops. I'd appreciate it if you could share
your feedback on the request fulfillment process
to help us improve our services.

Regards,
Priya Sharma
Service Desk Analyst
```

Response from Pooja Shah:

- **Subject:** Feedback: Laptop Fulfillment – RF-2024-1125
- **From:** Pooja Shah
- **To:** Priya Sharma
- **Content:**

```
Hi Priya,

The request fulfillment process was smooth and
timely. I particularly appreciate the constant
updates and partial delivery arrangement. Thank
you for the excellent service!

Regards,
Pooja Shah
```

Outcome

The request was fulfilled within the stipulated time frame, ensuring that the R&D team at Srishti Pharmaceuticals could begin their project on schedule. The proactive communication and collaboration between teams highlighted ABCD solution efficiency in request fulfillment.

Case Study: Access Management at ACD Solutions

Background

ABCD Solutions, an IT service provider based in Bengaluru, manages IT infrastructure for Shakti Finance Ltd., a leading financial services company headquartered in Mumbai. Shakti Finance's HR team requested access for a new employee to critical

HR and payroll systems. This was a priority request as the new employee, Ananya Iyer, was scheduled to begin onboarding tasks immediately.

Request Overview

Request Details:

- **Request ID:** AM-2024-1234
- **Requester:** Meera Joshi, HR Manager, Shakti Finance Ltd.
- **Requirement:** Provision of system access to Ananya Iyer (new hire) for HRMS and Payroll portals.
- **Deadline:** Same day.

Access Management Process Timeline with Communications

Day 1: Request Submission

Email from Meera Joshi:

- **Subject:** Access Request for New Employee - Ananya Iyer
- **From:** Meera Joshi
- **To:** Priya Sharma (Service Desk Analyst)
- **Content:**

```markdown
Copy code
Hi Priya,
```

Please grant access to the following systems for our new employee, Ananya Iyer, who is joining today:

1. HRMS (Human Resources Management System)
2. Payroll Portal

Employee Details:

- Name: Ananya Iyer
- Employee ID: SF12345
- Role: HR Executive
- Department: Human Resources

Please confirm once access is provisioned.

Regards,
Meera Joshi
HR Manager, Shakti Finance Ltd.

Acknowledgment Email from Priya Sharma:

- **Subject:** Request Acknowledged: AM-2024-1234
- **From:** Priya Sharma
- **To:** Meera Joshi
- **Content:**

Hi Meera,

Thank you for your request. The request ID for tracking is AM-2024-1234.

I will coordinate with the relevant teams to provision access for Ananya Iyer and will keep you updated.

Regards,
Priya Sharma
Service Desk Analyst

Day 1: Validation and Approval

Internal Email from Priya Sharma to Access Management Team:

- **Subject:** Access Provisioning: New Hire - AM-2024-1234
- **From:** Priya Sharma
- **To:** Arjun Desai (Access Management Lead), Sneha Iyer (System Administrator)
- **Content:**

```
Hi Arjun and Sneha,

Please find below the details for access
provisioning:

- Employee Name: Ananya Iyer
- Employee ID: SF12345
- Role: HR Executive
- Systems Required: HRMS, Payroll Portal

Kindly validate and confirm if approvals are
required from any additional stakeholders.

Regards,
Priya Sharma
```

Approval Confirmation Email from Arjun Desai:

- **Subject:** Re: Access Provisioning: New Hire - AM-2024-1234
- **From:** Arjun Desai
- **To:** Priya Sharma

- **Content:**

```
Hi Priya,

HRMS and Payroll Portal access for HR employees
require approval from the IT Security Manager.
Please forward the request to Ramesh Naik (IT
Security Manager) for validation.

Regards,
Arjun Desai
```

Email from Priya Sharma to Ramesh Naik:

- **Subject:** Approval Request: Access Provisioning for Ananya Iyer
- **From:** Priya Sharma
- **To:** Ramesh Naik (IT Security Manager)
- **Content:**

```
Hi Ramesh,

Please approve access provisioning for the
following employee:

—  Name: Ananya Iyer
—  Employee ID: SF12345
—  Role: HR Executive
—  Access Required: HRMS and Payroll Portal

Regards,
Priya Sharma
```

Approval Email from Ramesh Naik:

- **Subject:** Re: Approval Request: Access Provisioning for Ananya Iyer

- **From:** Ramesh Naik
- **To:** Priya Sharma, Arjun Desai
- **Content:**

```
Hi Priya,

Approved. Please proceed with the access
provisioning.

Regards,
Ramesh Naik
```

Day 1: Access Provisioning

Phone Call:

- **Priya Sharma to Sneha Iyer**

    - **Priya:** "Sneha, the access request for Ananya Iyer has been approved by Ramesh Naik. Could you provision the required access today?"
    - **Sneha:** "Sure, Priya. I'll complete it within the next two hours and update you."

Email from Sneha Iyer:

- **Subject:** Access Provisioning Completed: AM-2024-1234
- **From:** Sneha Iyer
- **To:** Priya Sharma, Meera Joshi
- **Content:**

```
Hi Priya and Meera,

Access to HRMS and Payroll Portal has been
successfully provisioned for Ananya Iyer.

Login Details:

-  Username: ananya.iyer@shaktifinance.com
-  Temporary Password: [Sent to Ananya's
   registered email]

Please let me know if further assistance is
required.

Regards,
Sneha Iyer
System Administrator
```

Day 1: Confirmation and Closure

Email from Meera Joshi:

- **Subject:** Access Request Completed: AM-2024-1234
- **From:** Meera Joshi
- **To:** Priya Sharma, Sneha Iyer
- **Content:**

```
Hi Priya and Sneha,

Thank you for the prompt provisioning of access
for Ananya Iyer. She has confirmed that she can
log in and access the required systems.

Regards,
Meera Joshi
```

Closure Email from Priya Sharma:

- **Subject:** Request Closed: AM-2024-1234
- **From:** Priya Sharma
- **To:** Meera Joshi
- **Content:**

```
Hi Meera,

Thank you for confirming. The request AM-2024-
1234 is now closed. Please feel free to reach
out for any further assistance.

Regards,
Priya Sharma
Service Desk Analyst
```

Outcome

The access request was completed successfully on the same day, ensuring that Ananya Iyer could begin her work without any delays. The seamless communication between the HR, IT, and Access Management teams highlighted the efficiency of ABCD solution Access Management process.

Closure:

The access request ticket was officially closed on October 6th, with all details recorded in the access management system for future reference.

1. Lessons Learned from Challenges

Lessons learned from IT service desk challenges include the importance of proactive communication, efficient incident management, and continuous training. For example, regular updates during major outages build trust, streamlined processes reduce resolution times, and ongoing training ensures staff can handle new technologies and complex issues effectively.

Common Pitfalls of IT Service Desk and How to Avoid Them

1. **Inadequate Training:**

   - **Pitfall:** Service desk analysts are not sufficiently trained on new software or updates, leading to prolonged resolution times and frustrated users.

   - **Example:** A new CRM system was implemented, but analysts were not trained properly, resulting in numerous unresolved tickets.

   - **Solution:** Implement continuous training programs and refresher courses whenever new systems or updates are introduced. Schedule regular training sessions and provide access to updated resources and documentation.

2. **Poor Communication:**

   - **Pitfall:** Lack of clear communication between the IT service desk and users, causing confusion and dissatisfaction.

   - **Example:** During a major network outage, users were not informed about the issue or the expected resolution time, leading to multiple redundant calls and emails.

   - **Solution:** Establish a communication protocol that includes regular updates to users during major incidents. Use multiple channels (emails, intranet, SMS) to keep users informed about the status and expected resolution times.

3. **Inefficient Incident Management:**

   - **Pitfall:** Incidents are not prioritized correctly, resulting in critical issues being overlooked.

   - **Example:** A critical server issue was placed in the same queue as minor user requests, delaying its resolution and causing significant downtime.

   - **Solution:** Implement a robust incident management system that prioritizes tickets based on their impact and urgency. Train analysts to recognize and escalate critical issues promptly.

4. **Lack of Documentation:**

   - **Pitfall:** Incomplete or outdated documentation leads to inconsistent troubleshooting and resolution processes.

- ○ **Example:** Without proper documentation, analysts struggled to resolve recurring issues, leading to repeated downtime and user frustration.

- ○ **Solution:** Maintain a comprehensive knowledge base with updated documentation on common issues and resolutions. Encourage analysts to contribute to and regularly update this knowledge base.

5. **Ignoring Feedback:**

- ○ **Pitfall:** Not collecting or acting on user feedback, resulting in repeated issues and declining user satisfaction.

- ○ **Example:** Users repeatedly reported slow response times, but no action was taken to investigate or resolve the underlying issues.

- ○ **Solution:** Implement a feedback system to collect user input regularly. Analyze feedback to identify common issues and areas for improvement and take corrective actions to address them.

6. **Over-Reliance on Manual Processes:**

- ○ **Pitfall:** Excessive manual processes slow down resolution times and increase the risk of human error.

- ○ **Example:** Analysts manually logged each incident, leading to delays and inconsistent data entry.

- ○ **Solution:** Automate repetitive tasks such as ticket logging, prioritization, and routing. Utilize automated tools to streamline workflows and reduce the risk of errors.

Chapter Summary – Mindmap

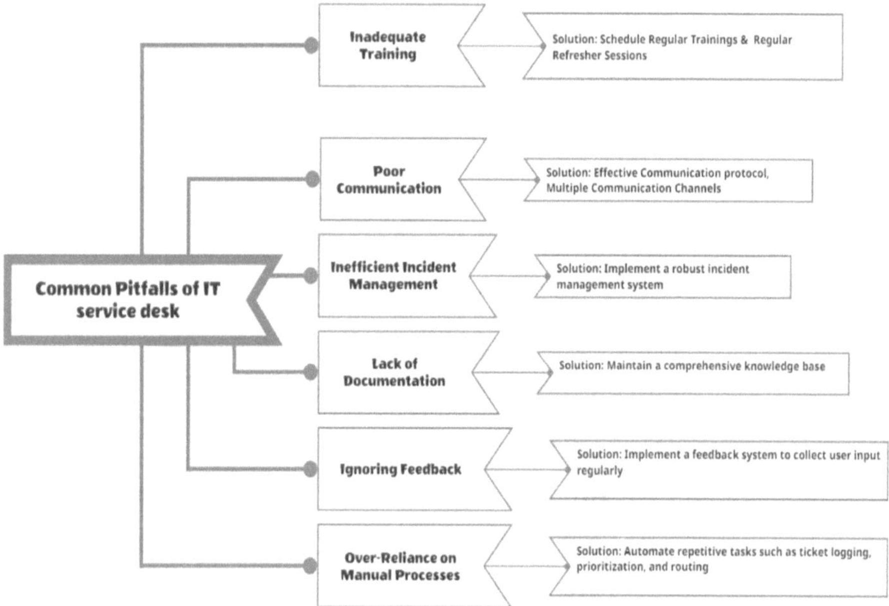

Conclusion

Recap and Final Thoughts

In managing a 24x7 IT service desk, it's crucial to address staffing, shift handovers, training, communication, and employee well-being.

Leveraging automation and maintaining consistent service quality are key to efficiency. Regularly collecting customer feedback and ensuring effective incident management enhance satisfaction and reliability.

Planning for scalability and adopting flexible staffing models prepare the service desk for growth and increased demand.

By understanding and avoiding common pitfalls, you can ensure a smooth operation, boost team morale, and achieve exceptional customer service.

This book provides practical strategies and insights to help you build and manage a successful 24x7 IT service desk.

Key Takeaways –

1. **Strategic Staffing and Scheduling:**

    ○ Implement balanced and flexible shift schedules to prevent burnout and ensure adequate coverage.

    ○ Use cross-training to enhance team flexibility and effectiveness.

2. **Effective Shift Handover:**

   - Establish clear, structured handover processes and documentation to ensure smooth transitions between shifts.

3. **Continuous Training and Development:**

   - Provide comprehensive onboarding and ongoing training to keep staff updated on best practices and new technologies.

   - Encourage cross-training to diversify skills.

4. **Leveraging Automation and Tools:**

   - Utilize automation for routine tasks, ticket management, and incident monitoring to increase efficiency.

   - Keep systems and tools up-to-date and integrated for seamless operations.

5. **Consistent Service Quality:**

   - Develop and enforce standardized procedures to ensure consistent handling of issues across all shifts.

   - Conduct regular quality audits and reviews to maintain high service standards.

6. **Proactive Communication and Collaboration:**

   - Use effective communication tools and hold regular team meetings to ensure all team members are informed and aligned.

- Implement feedback mechanisms for continuous improvement.

7. **Employee Well-being and Engagement:**

   - Promote work-life balance and provide support programs to maintain high morale and productivity.
   - Recognize and reward employees to boost retention and satisfaction.

8. **Customer-Centric Approach:**

   - Implement self-service options and maintain a customer-centric approach to enhance customer satisfaction.
   - Regularly collect and act on customer feedback to improve service quality.

9. **Robust Incident Management:**

   - Develop clear incident management protocols and train staff accordingly.
   - Use automated alerts and conduct post-incident analyses to prevent future issues.

10. **Scalability and Flexibility:**

    - Plan for scalability by investing in scalable solutions and infrastructure.
    - Use flexible staffing models to effectively manage peak times and growth.

Encouragement for New Service Desk Managers

Embarking on your journey as a service desk manager, especially in a 24x7 environment, can be both challenging and rewarding. Remember, the key to success lies in your ability to adapt, learn, and lead with empathy and foresight. Here are some words of encouragement as you step into this pivotal role:

1. **Embrace Learning:** Every challenge is an opportunity to learn and grow. Stay curious, seek knowledge, and continuously improve your skills and understanding of the industry.

2. **Lead with Empathy:** Your team is your greatest asset. Foster a supportive environment where team members feel valued, heard, and motivated. Empathy and strong communication are your tools for building a cohesive and resilient team.

3. **Stay Adaptable:** The IT landscape is ever-changing. Be prepared to adapt and evolve with new technologies and methodologies. Flexibility and a proactive approach will keep your service desk ahead of the curve.

4. **Leverage Technology:** Utilize automation and advanced tools to enhance efficiency and accuracy. These resources will help streamline operations and free up time for more strategic tasks.

5. **Prioritize Quality:** Consistent, high-quality service is the cornerstone of customer satisfaction. Develop and enforce standards and procedures that ensure excellence in every interaction.

6. **Focus on Well-being:** The well-being of your team directly impacts performance and morale. Promote work-life balance, provide necessary support, and recognize achievements to keep your team engaged and productive.

7. **Foster Continuous Improvement:** Always seek feedback from both customers and your team. Use this feedback to drive continuous improvement in processes, service quality, and team development.

8. **Celebrate Successes:** Acknowledge and celebrate both big and small successes. Recognizing achievements boosts morale and motivates your team to strive for excellence.

Remember, as a service desk manager, you play a crucial role in ensuring smooth operations and customer satisfaction. Your leadership can transform challenges into opportunities and drive your team towards success. Stay positive, stay determined, and know that your efforts make a significant impact. Welcome to the exciting world of 24x7 IT service desk management!

Glossary of Terms

- **Incident:** An unplanned interruption or reduction in the quality of an IT service.

- **Service Request:** A user request for information, advice, or a standard change.

- **Change Management:** The process of managing changes to the IT environment.

- **Problem:** The underlying cause of one or more incidents.

- **Root Cause Analysis (RCA):** A method of identifying the root causes of problems or incidents.

- **Service Level Agreement (SLA):** A formal agreement between an IT service provider and a customer defining the level of service expected.

- **Operational Level Agreement (OLA):** An agreement between an IT service provider and another part of the same organization.

- **Key Performance Indicator (KPI):** A measurable value that demonstrates how effectively an IT service is achieving key business objectives.

- **Ticket:** A record of an incident, problem, service request, or change.

- **Knowledge Base:** A repository of information, solutions, and best practices.

- **Escalation:** The process of involving higher-level support to resolve an issue.

- **First Call Resolution (FCR):** Resolving a customer's issue on the first contact.

- **Response Time:** The time taken to respond to a ticket.

- **Resolution Time:** The time taken to resolve a ticket.

- **Priority:** The relative importance of an incident or service request, typically based on its impact and urgency.

- **Impact:** The effect an incident has on the business.

- **Urgency:** The required speed of resolution.

- **Availability:** The ability of an IT service or component to perform its function when required.

- **Downtime:** The period when an IT service is not available.

- **Service Desk:** The single point of contact between the service provider and the users.

- **Incident Management:** The process of managing the lifecycle of all incidents.

- **Problem Management:** The process of managing the lifecycle of all problems.

- **Change Request (CR):** A formal proposal for an alteration to some aspect of the IT environment.

- **Configuration Management Database (CMDB):** A database used to manage the configuration items.

- **Release Management:** The process of managing, planning, and controlling the release of new or changed services.

- **Event Management:** The process of monitoring all events that occur through the IT infrastructure.

- **Service Catalog:** A structured document with information about all live IT services.

- **Business Continuity Plan (BCP):** A plan to continue business operations in case of a disaster.

- **Disaster Recovery (DR):** The process of recovering from a disaster.

- **User:** An individual who uses the IT services.

- **Service Owner:** The individual responsible for the delivery of a specific IT service.

- **Incident Commander:** The person responsible for managing the response to a major incident.

- **Service Portfolio:** The complete set of services managed by a service provider.

- **Major Incident:** A high-impact, urgent incident that requires a coordinated response.

- **ITIL (Information Technology Infrastructure Library):** A set of practices for IT service management.

- **Monitoring and Event Management:** The practice of systematically observing services and components.

- **Service Desk Analyst (SDA):** A frontline staff member who provides IT support.

- **Service Desk Manager:** The person responsible for managing the service desk.

- **Service Desk Lead:** A senior member of the service desk team who provides guidance and support.

- **SPOC (Single Point of Contact):** A single channel for all user communication.

- **Knowledge Management:** The process of sharing perspectives, ideas, experience, and information.

- **Configuration Item (CI):** Any component that needs to be managed in order to deliver an IT service.

- **Business Impact Analysis (BIA):** A process that identifies and evaluates the potential effects of an interruption.

- **Service Improvement Plan (SIP):** A formal plan to improve IT services and processes.

- **Root Cause:** The original cause of an incident or problem.

- **Workaround:** A temporary solution to reduce or eliminate the impact of an incident or problem.

- **Backlog:** A list of incidents, problems, or service requests that have not yet been addressed.

- **Service Window:** A period of time when maintenance can be performed.

- **Call Logging:** The process of recording details about incidents or requests.

- **Ticketing System:** Software used to track and manage incidents, problems, and service requests.

References

Resources for Further Learning

Recommended Books, Courses, and Certifications

As you continue your journey in managing a 24x7 IT service desk, ongoing learning and professional development are crucial. Here are some valuable resources to deepen your knowledge and stay updated with the latest trends and best practices in the field:

Books Reference

- **"The Help Desk Handbook: Learn How to Setup and Run a Successful Help Desk" by Paul Glen**: A comprehensive guide to setting up and managing a successful help desk operation.

- **"ITIL Foundation: ITIL 4 Edition" by AXELOS**: Essential reading for understanding ITIL principles and practices that are critical for effective IT service management.

- **"Measuring ITIL: Measuring, Reporting and Modeling – the IT Service Management Metrics that Matter Most to IT Senior Executives" by Randy A. Steinberg**: Focuses on metrics and performance measurement in IT service management.

Online Courses

- **Coursera – "IT Support Professional Certificate" by Google**: A series of courses that provide a foundation in IT support, including customer service, troubleshooting, and networking.

- **Udemy – "ITIL 4 Foundation Exam Preparation"**: Prepares you for the ITIL 4 Foundation exam, covering key concepts and practices.

- **LinkedIn Learning – "IT Service Desk: Management Fundamentals"**: Offers insights into managing a service desk, including team management and customer service.

Professional Certifications

- **ITIL Certification**: The Information Technology Infrastructure Library (ITIL) certification is essential for understanding and implementing IT service management best practices.

- **HDI Support Center Manager Certification**: Provides knowledge and skills necessary to manage a service desk effectively, focusing on leadership and performance management.

- **CompTIA A+ Certification**: Covers essential IT skills and is a foundational certification for IT support roles.

Industry Websites and Blogs

- **HDI (Help Desk Institute)**: Offers resources, articles, and best practices for IT support professionals.

- **ITSM.Tools**: Provides insights, articles, and resources on IT service management.

- **TechTarget – SearchITOperations**: Covers the latest news, trends, and best practices in IT operations and service management.

Forums and Communities

- **Reddit – r/ITCareerQuestions**: A community where you can ask questions and share experiences with other IT professionals.

- **Spiceworks Community**: A platform for IT professionals to discuss issues, share solutions, and network with peers.

- **IT Service Management Forum (itSMF)**: A global community of IT service management professionals, offering events, publications, and networking opportunities.